YOU CH

THE TROJAN WAR

AN INTERACTIVE MYTHOLOGICAL ADVENTURE

by Blake Hoena
illustrated by Nadine Takvorian

Consultant: Dr. Laurel Bowman
Department of Greek and Roman Studies
University of Victoria
Victoria, BC, Canada

CAPSTONE PRESS
a capstone imprint

You Choose Books are published by Capstone Press,
1710 Roe Crest Drive, North Mankato, Minnesota 56003
www.mycapstone.com

Copyright © 2017 by Capstone Press, a Capstone imprint. All rights reserved. No part of this publication may be reproduced in whole or in part, or stored in a retrieval system, or transmitted in any form or by any means, electronic, mechanical, photocopying, recording, or otherwise, without written permission of the publisher.

Library of Congress Cataloging-in-Publication Data
Names: Hoena, B. A., author.
Title: The Trojan War : an interactive mythological adventure / by Blake Hoena.
Description: North Mankato, Minnesota : Capstone Press, 2017. | Series: You choose books. Ancient Greek myths. | Includes bibliographical references and index. Identifiers: LCCN 2016039230
ISBN 9781515748229 (library binding) | ISBN 9781515748274 (pbk.) ISBN 9781515748311 (ebook PDF)
Subjects: LCSH: Trojan War—Juvenile literature. | Mythology, Greek—Juvenile literature. | Plot-your-own stories.
Classification: LCC BL793.T7 H64 2017 | DDC 398.20938—dc23
LC record available at https://lccn.loc.gov/2016039230

Editorial Credits
Mandy Robbins, editor, Ted Williams, designer;
Kelly Garvin, media researcher, Katy LaVigne, production specialist

IIlustrations by Nadine Takvorian

Photo Credits:
Shutterstock/siete_vidas, 104

Artistic elements: Shutterstock: Alex Novikov, Eky Studio, reyhan, Samira Dragonfly, Tymonko Galyna,

Printed and bound in Canada.
010050S17

Table of Contents

About Your Adventure 5

Chapter 1: A Dangerous Prophecy 7

Chapter 2: The Heroes of Troy 15

Chapter 3: Achilles and Patroclus..........41

Chapter 4: The Heroes of Greece 75

Chapter 5: The Real City of Troy 105

Greek Gods and Goddesses 107

Other Paths to Explore 108

Read More 109

Internet Sites............................. 109

Glossary 110

Bibliography 111

Index..................................... 112

About Your Adventure

YOU are a mighty hero caught up in the brutal Trojan War. You must pick sides and try to win the war. Will you be able to help solve the conflict between the Greeks and Trojans and make it out of battle alive?

Chapter One sets the scene. Then you choose which path to take. Follow the directions at the bottom of each page. The choices you make determine what happens next. After you finish your path, go back and read the others for more adventures.

YOU CHOOSE the path you take through this mythical adventure.

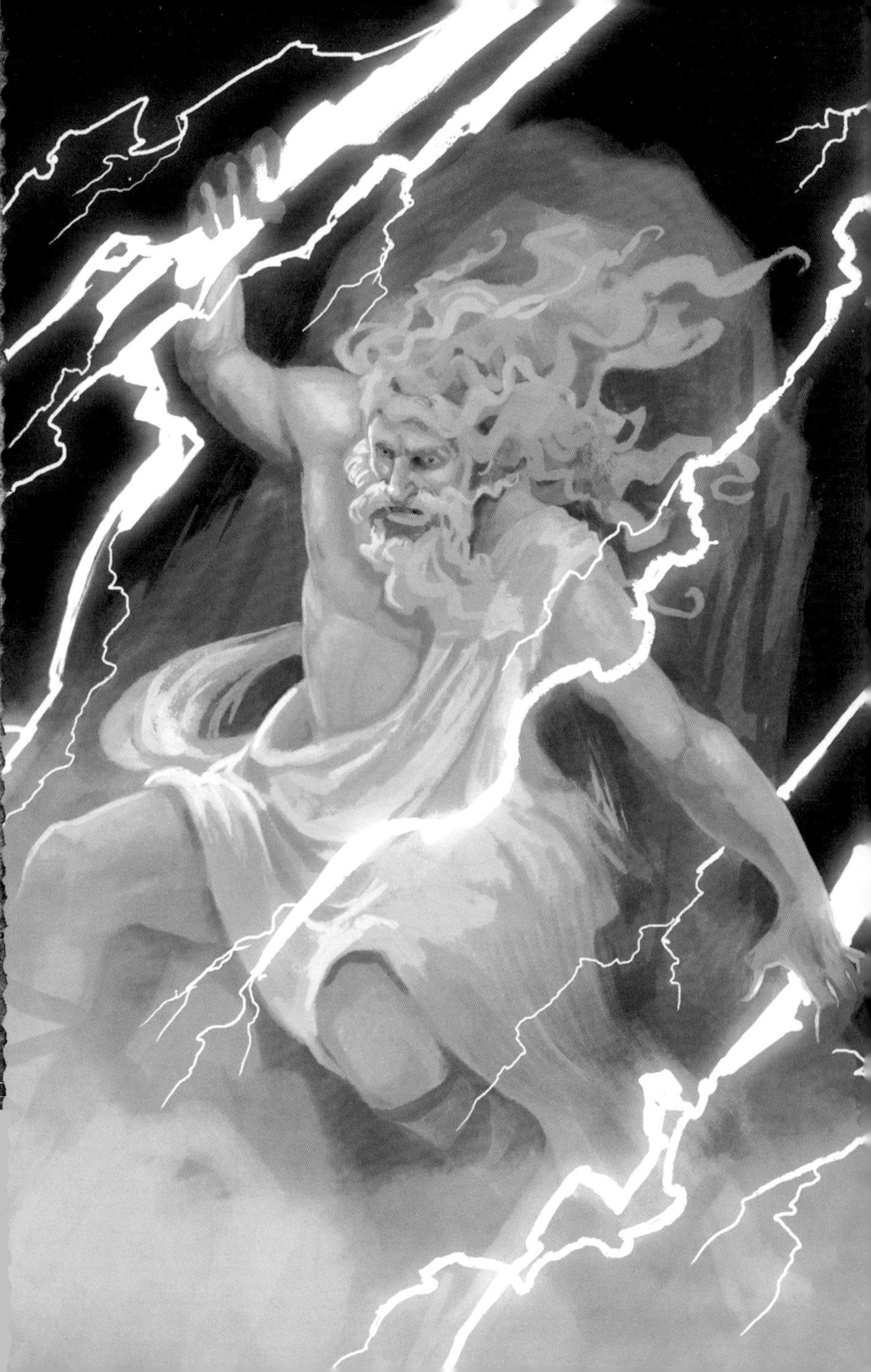

Chapter 1

A Dangerous Prophecy

Zeus sits on his throne high up on Mount Olympus. He is god of the sky and ruler over all of the other Greek gods. From his throne, he watches for threats to his rule in the world below.

Many gods and mortals have challenged him. He was once confronted by Typhon, a giant monster with snakes for legs who breathed volcanic ash. But Typhon could not defeat the mighty ruler of the gods. Zeus also defended Mount Olympus from an army of giants. Even his fellow Olympians have tried to overthrow him. But no god, monster, or mortal has succeeded in taking his throne — at least not yet.

Turn the page.

Suddenly, Poseidon appears at Zeus's side. He is the god of the sea and Zeus's brother.

"Turn your watchful gaze to the island of Lemnos," Poseidon says.

From his throne, Zeus sees the sea nymph Thetis. She sits on a sandy beach talking to her father, Nereus. He is the ancient god known as the Old Man of the Sea. Anything Nereus has to say is worth listening to. He has a knack for knowing things that might come to pass.

"Bear a child, fair goddess," Nereus says to his daughter. "And you shall be the mother of a youth whose deeds and might shall surpass his father's."

Nereus's words worry Zeus. Any child born to Thetis would be more powerful than her husband. If Thetis marries a god, her son could grow up to be mightier than Zeus himself.

"Any godly child of Thetis could threaten your rule," Poseidon says, in a panic. "That could mean trouble for all of us Olympians!"

"Then she must marry a mortal," Zeus replies.

"But who?" Poseidon asks. "She is a Nereid. She won't want to marry just any man."

"He will need to be a great hero," Zeus says.

Zeus turns his gaze to Mount Pelion, where the wise old Centaur Chiron lives. Chiron has trained heroes, from Hercules to Theseus, in the art of combat. Today, he is training with Peleus, one of the heroes who traveled with Jason and the Argonauts in search of the Golden Fleece. He will do just fine.

Zeus sends word to Peleus that he is to marry Thetis. Not wanting to anger the powerful god, Peleus agrees.

Turn the page.

Peleus sails to the island of Lemnos and waits for Thetis on the beach. Peleus sees her swim to shore and sit on a piece of driftwood. He quietly sneaks up and wraps his arms around her.

But Thetis is a shape shifter. She becomes a lioness, roaring and clawing at Peleus. He does not let go. Then Thetis turns into a snake and tries to bite Peleus. Still, he holds on. Finally she becomes a shark and thrashes wildly. Peleus does not loosen his grip. Eventually, Thetis gives up her struggle and takes the form of a woman.

"What do you want from me?" she asks.

"Your hand in marriage," he replies.

Thetis knows they are destined to have a mighty son, so she accepts Peleus's proposal. Their wedding is held on Mount Pelion. All of the gods are invited, except for Eris, goddess of strife.

Eris tries to sneak into the wedding, but Zeus catches her.

"You are not welcome here," Zeus says.

She points at three goddesses sitting at a table.

"But you invited Athena, Aphrodite, and Hera," Eris says. "Let me join them. I'll behave."

"No," Zeus replies. "You only cause trouble. If you do not leave, I will force you out."

"If I must," Eris scowls. "But first . . ."

Eris tosses a golden apple onto the table where the three goddesses sit. Then she disappears.

Hera, the goddess of home and marriage, reaches over to pick up the apple. The words "To the Fairest" are inscribed on it.

Turn the page.

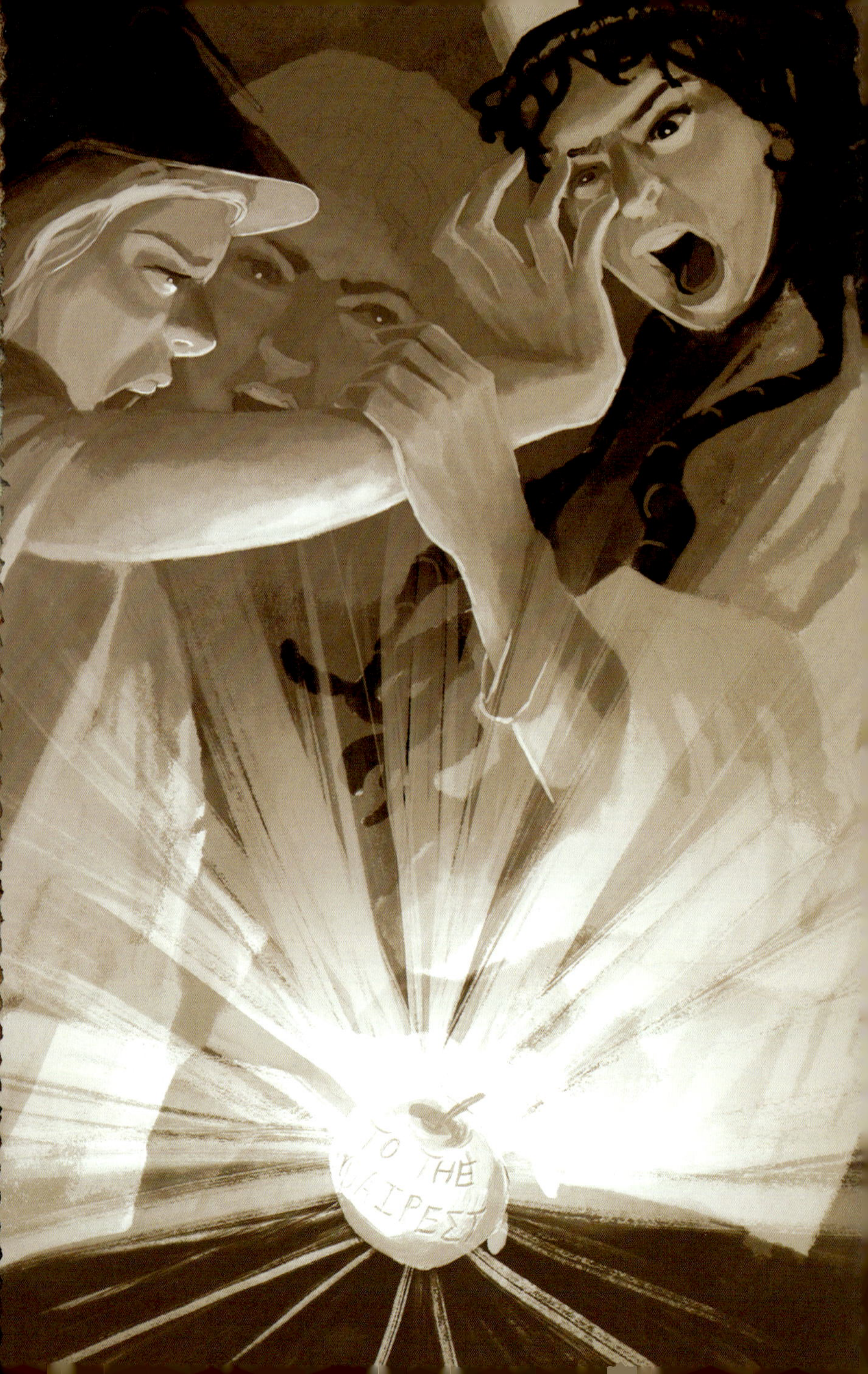
TO THE

Athena, goddess of wisdom, takes the apple from Hera and says, "It must be meant for me."

"I am the fairest, without a doubt," says Aphrodite, the goddess of love.

Soon, the three goddesses are shouting at each other over who deserves the apple. And when gods argue, people suffer. The disagreement leads to one of the greatest wars recorded in myth. The Trojan War pits a large Greek army against the mighty city of Troy. Gods pick sides in the conflict, and the mightiest heroes of the day take to the battlefield. Which side will you take? Which hero will you be?

> To be a Trojan Hero, go to page 15.
>
> To be Thetis and Peleus's future son, go to page 41.
>
> To be a Greek Hero, go to page 75.

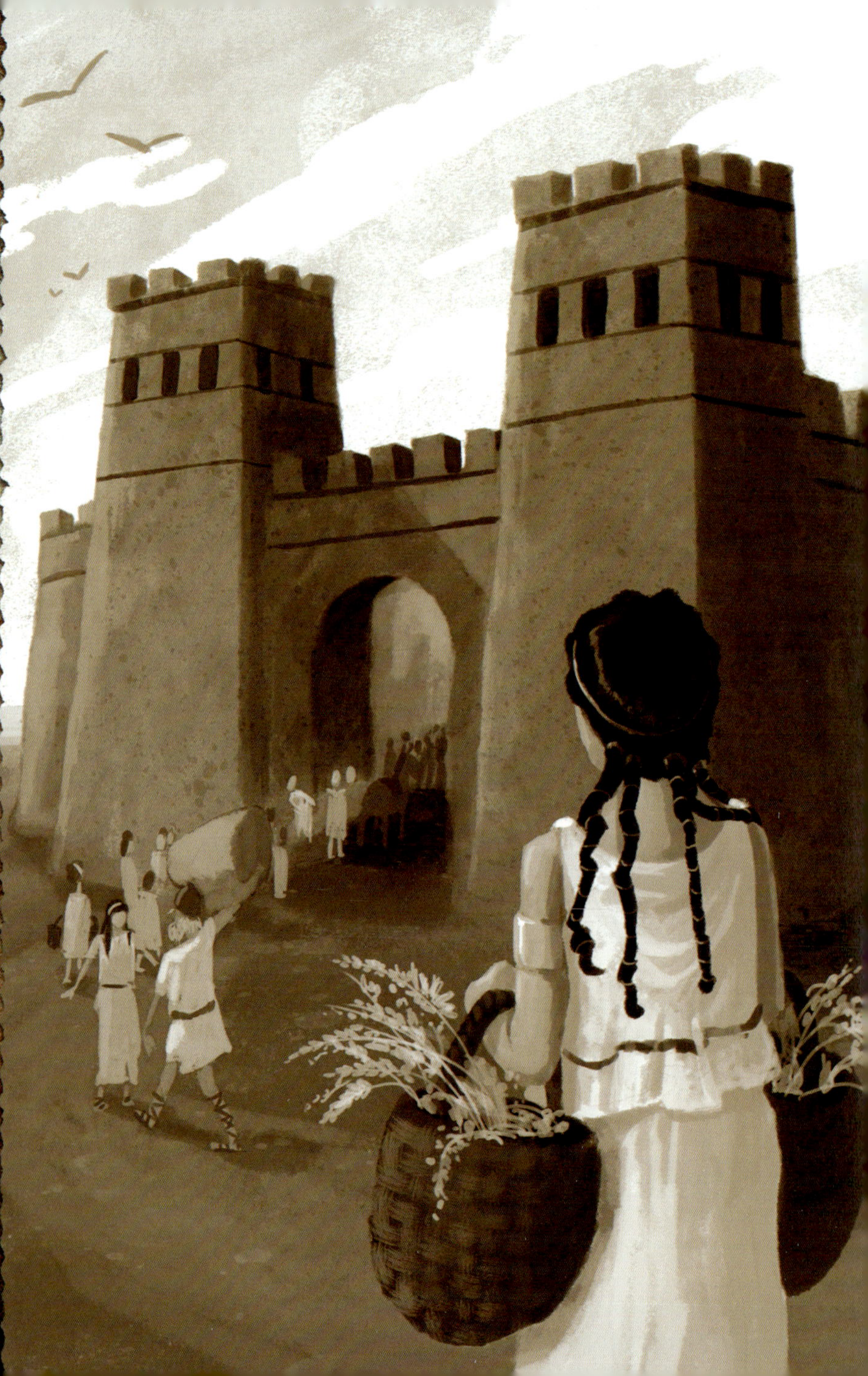

Chapter 2

The Heroes of Troy

The kingdom of Troy is a powerful and wealthy city on the Aegean Sea. King Ilium built Troy around 3000 BCE. He prayed for guidance, and the magical Palladium dropped from the sky. This small wooden statue was a gift from Athena. It is said to protect the city from invaders.

Troy's most stunning features are its outer walls. They were said to be built by the gods. According to myth, Poseidon and Apollo had once planned to overthrow Zeus. Zeus punished the two gods by forcing them to serve Troy's King Laomedon for a year. The king asked the gods to build walls that could never be brought down.

Turn the page.

Sections of wall are connected by five massive towers. Each tower defends one of the gates to the city.

Troy's might and wealth rival that of any Greek city. At the time of Peleus and Thetis's wedding, King Priam and Queen Hecuba ruled Troy. Within the kingdom lived heroes equal to those of Greece. One was King Priam's son Paris, and another was Aeneas, a distant relative of the king's.

> To be Paris, go to page 17.
> To be Aeneas, turn to page 19.

While pregnant with you, Queen Hecuba dreamt of a flaming child. Not knowing what this meant, she sought out the seer Aesacus. He told your mother that you would be Troy's doom. So when you were born, King Priam and Queen Hecuba sent you away. You were raised by a herdsman on Mount Ida, far away from Troy.

Years later, you stand on a mountain slope tending your herd. Suddenly, Hermes, the messenger of the gods, appears before you.

"The mighty Zeus commands you to make the choice," he says, handing you a golden apple.

You are confused. As you turn the apple around in your hands, you notice the words "To the Fairest" inscribed on it. You look up to ask the god what it means. But instead of Hermes, three goddesses now stand before you.

Turn the page.

You gulp nervously. You have just been asked by the ruler of the gods to make an impossible choice. Three powerful goddesses look at you expectantly. You are to choose who is the fairest.

"If you pick me," the motherly Hera says, "you will rule over a vast kingdom and have extreme wealth."

"If you pick me," the wise Athena says," you will be skilled in combat and always victorious in battle."

"If you pick me," the lovely Aphrodite says, "you will marry the most beautiful woman in the world."

To choose Hera, turn to page 22.
To choose Athena, turn to page 23.
To choose Aphrodite, turn to page 24.

Aphrodite, the goddess of love, enjoyed tricking gods into falling in love with mortals. But she had made the mistake of playing this trick on Zeus. He got his revenge by making Aphrodite fall in love with a mortal man, Anchises. He was a herdsman on Mount Ida and was a distant relative of King Priam of Troy. He and Aphrodite are your parents.

After your birth, Anchises raises you. You're a mortal, so you cannot live with your mother atop Mount Olympus. But she vows to protect you.

With a goddess as a mother and a powerful king in your family, great things are expected of you. You more than meet those expectations. Through your bravery and skill on the battlefield, you become king of Dardania, a small kingdom near Troy.

Turn the page.

One day, a messenger from Troy visits you.

"Troy is under attack by a Greek army," he tells you. "King Priam requests your help."

You have heard that the Trojan prince Paris stole Helen, the most beautiful woman in the world, from her husband, King Menelaus of Sparta. Menelaus gathered an army of Greek heroes to attack Troy and get his wife back.

You're certain your mother had something to do with this, but going to war over a love affair seems foolish. You send the messenger away and refuse to help.

You think this will be the end of the matter, but you are wrong. One day, as you are out tending your cattle, a Greek raiding party confronts you.

"How dare you attack my lands!" you shout to the leader of the party. "It is Troy that you are at war with, not Dardania."

"I am Achilles," the man says. "And I have been ordered to raid these lands for supplies."

You cannot allow Achilles to attack your lands and steal your cattle. You are about to reach for your sword when Achilles knocks you down.

"I am taking your cattle," he says. "And I will take your life too, if you try to stop me."

You are suddenly at his mercy and have no other choice but to flee.

You did not want to go to war. But now, you are not sure you can avoid it.

To stay and defend Dardania, turn to page 28.
To lead your troops to Troy, turn to page 29.

Hera is the goddess of home and marriage. She is also Zeus's wife. That makes her one of the most powerful Greek goddesses. You would hate to anger her. The kingdom of Troy is already vast, and you could make it even greater.

That is exactly what happens when you give the apple to Hera. After your father's death, you become king of Troy and expand its borders.

While Hera is the goddess of marriage, Aphrodite is the goddess of love. She keeps you from ever falling in love. You never marry or have children. You die without an heir to your throne.

After your death, lords from across the land fight for control of the kingdom. Eventually, it falls into ruins. Its greatness is forgotten over time.

THE END

To follow another path, turn to page 13.

To learn about the real city of Troy, turn to page 105.

Athena is the goddess of wisdom and the protector of heroes. You find her offer exciting. You could go on adventures like the heroes Hercules and Perseus did.

After giving the apple to Athena, you go on great quests and win battles everywhere you go. People talk of your great deeds all across the land.

But while Athena is the goddess of wisdom, Aphrodite is the goddess of love. She won't forgive you for giving the apple to Athena. You never fall in love, marry, or have children.

You are always victorious in your battles and pursuits, but one after another your friends all fall in battle. Eventually, you die of old age, alone and regretting your choice.

THE END

To follow another path, turn to page 13.

To learn about the real city of Troy, turn to page 105.

You give the golden apple to Aphrodite. She is the goddess of love and beauty, after all.

"You will marry Helen," Aphrodite says, "Zeus's daughter with Queen Leda."

You have heard rumors of Helen's remarkable beauty. But she is already married.

"What of her husband, King Menelaus of Sparta?" you ask the goddess.

"He is not as deserving as you," she says. "Only a daughter of Zeus is worthy of you."

You can't resist the goddess's power of persuasion. Under her guidance you sail to Sparta and sneak into the palace. You find doors unbarred and guards asleep. It is as if the goddess of love is seeing you safely through the palace.

When you step into Helen's room, you see fear in her eyes.

"It's okay," you say. "Aphrodite sent me here."

As you speak, Helen's face becomes calm. She too must be under Aphrodite's spell.

As though she is in a trance, Helen follows you down to the docks. Together, you board your ship and sail across the Aegean Sea. During the trip, you worry that Menelaus, Helen's husband, will be furious. He will probably send an army after you to get Helen back. But you and Helen are under Aphrodite's influence. Neither of you cares.

You are surprised, however, by the size of the force that attacks Troy. Hundreds of ships and thousands of Greek warriors wait outside the city walls. They are too many for the Trojans to repel but not enough to conquer the city. The standoff lasts for years.

Turn the page.

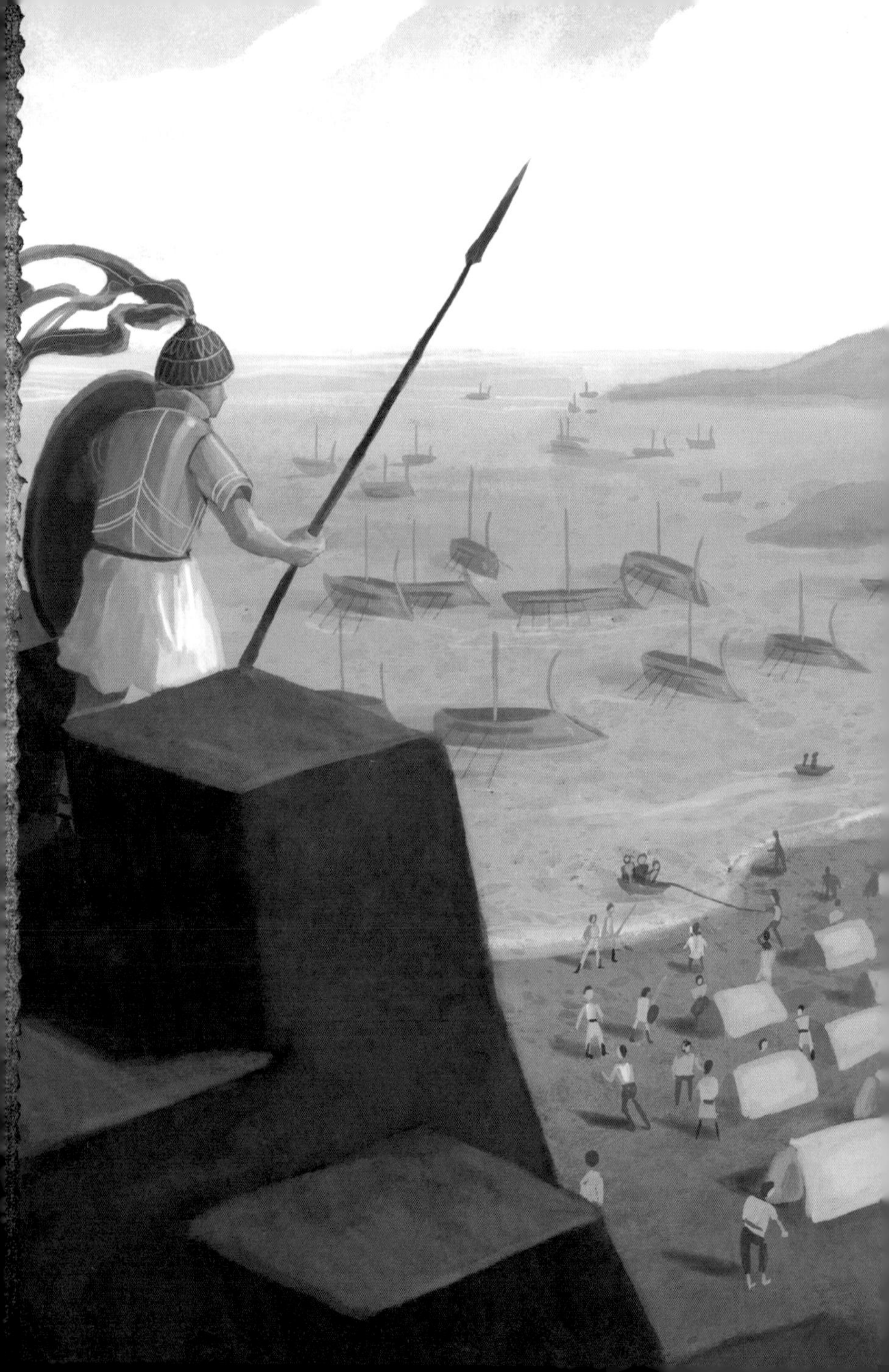

Finally, King Menelaus sends a messenger to speak with you in your father's throne room.

"Menelaus wishes to challenge you to a duel for Helen's return," he says.

"And if my son wins, Menelaus will leave our shores and Helen behind?" King Priam asks.

"He will," the messenger says.

"You must accept the challenge," your brother Hector says. He is leader of the Trojan army.

King Menelaus is a mighty warrior. You don't know if you can defeat him, but this is your best chance, not only to win Helen's place in your kingdom, but also to save Troy from destruction.

To accept the challenge, turn to page 33.
To refuse the challenge, turn to page 37.

After the attack by Achilles, you raise an army to guard your land. For a while you keep the Greek raiding parties out of Dardania. But as the war in Troy wages on, the Greeks get desperate for supplies. Achilles and his soldiers are back.

"You won't be taking my cattle today," you say.

"Then I must take your life," he replies.

Your kingdom's forces outnumber Achilles's men. But it seems that, no matter how many men he faces, he is never injured. As Achilles battles one of your men, you hurl a spear at him. But it bounces right off of him. Achilles launches the spear back at you. It sinks deep into your flesh. You fall to the ground and take your last breath.

THE END

To follow another path, turn to page 13.

To learn about the real city of Troy, turn to page 105.

You are infuriated by the raid on your lands, so you raise an army. You could stay in Dardania and just defend your kingdom. But as long as the Greeks are near Troy, raiding parties will attack Dardania. You must send the Greeks back to Greece. You march your army to Troy to help King Priam.

Your troops turn the tide of the war in Troy's favor. So Prince Hector, leader of the Trojan army, plans a daring attack.

"If we can destroy the Greek ships, their army will have no supplies or a way home," he says. "They would lose all hope of winning this war."

The king agrees. So one morning, the entire army gathers inside the main gate. When it opens, the Trojan forces charge out. They take the Greeks by surprise and fight their way toward the ships.

Turn the page.

As the battle rages, you see one of Greece's soldiers, Diomedes, rallying his troops. They start to push the Trojans back. You need to challenge him, or the Trojan army could lose the battle.

You hurl your spear at Diomedes, and he ducks it. He tosses his spear at you, and you knock it aside with your shield. You both draw your swords and attack. Clangs ring out with each blow. Suddenly he slices your hip. You stagger backward.

Diomedes raises his sword to deliver a fatal blow. But a flash of white light appears between you. It is Aphrodite, your mother. She snatches you from the battlefield, saving your life. You suddenly find yourself in the palace.

"What have you done?" you say in frustration. "I need to rejoin my forces."

Turn the page.

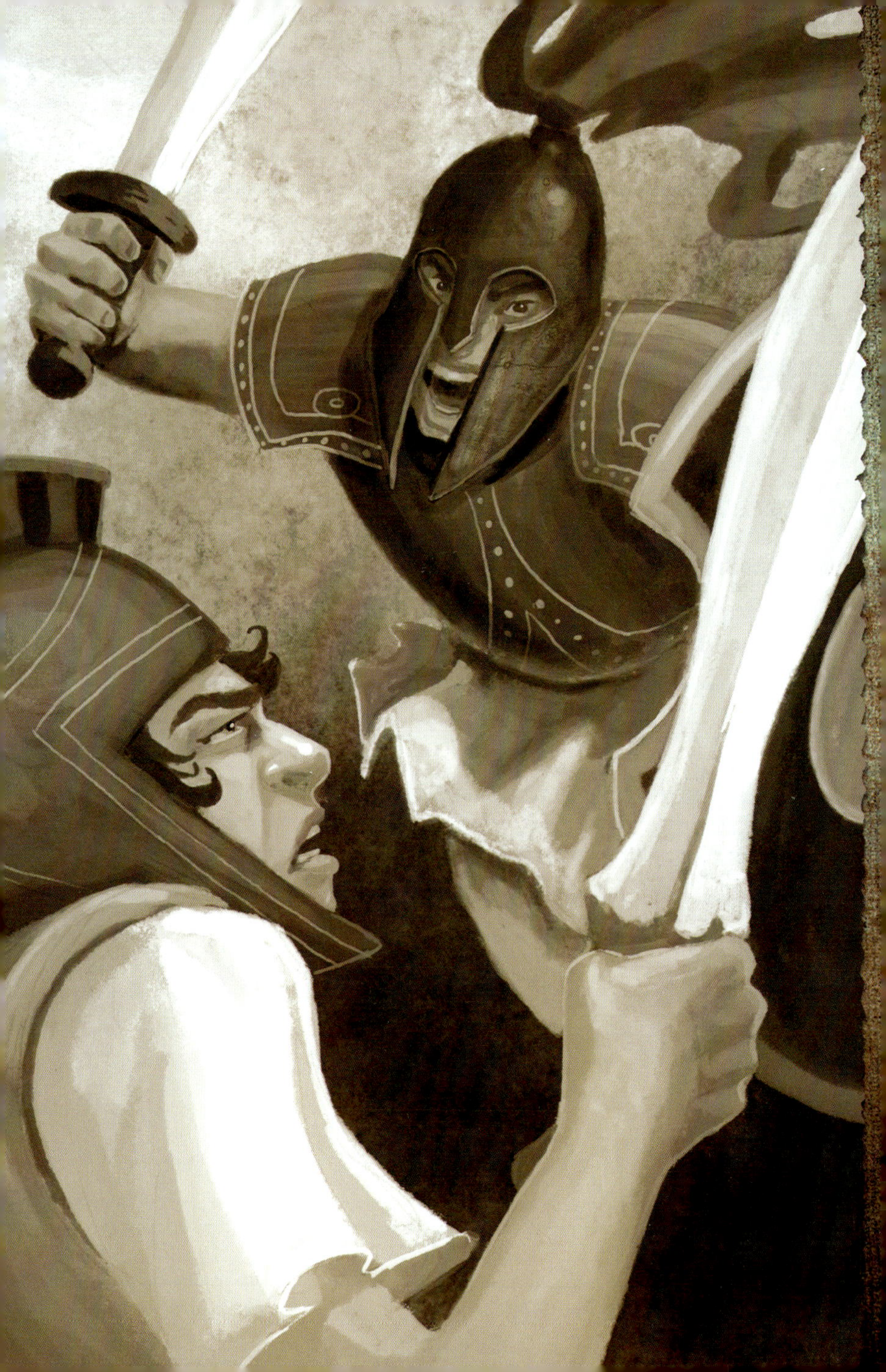

"You must leave! I beg you," your mother says. "Set sail across the Aegean Sea. I fear for your safety if you stay."

"But we are on the verge of winning this war," you plead.

> To rejoin your forces, turn to page 38.
> To leave Troy, turn to page 39.

You accept Menelaus's challenge. It only seems right. Stealing Helen away from him is what caused this war in the first place.

Your brother Hector straps on your armor and hands you your shield and spear. Then you march out of the city gates.

Menelaus is waiting for you. Like you, he is armed with a spear and shield. But unlike you, he walks with the confidence of a seasoned warrior. Then he charges. Menelaus thrusts his spear at you. You block it with your shield. Then you lunge with your spear, but Menelaus knocks it aside. You jab again with your spear. Instead of blocking it, Menelaus simply steps aside, avoiding the blow. Then he smashes his shield into yours. You fall backward. Your guard is down.

Turn the page.

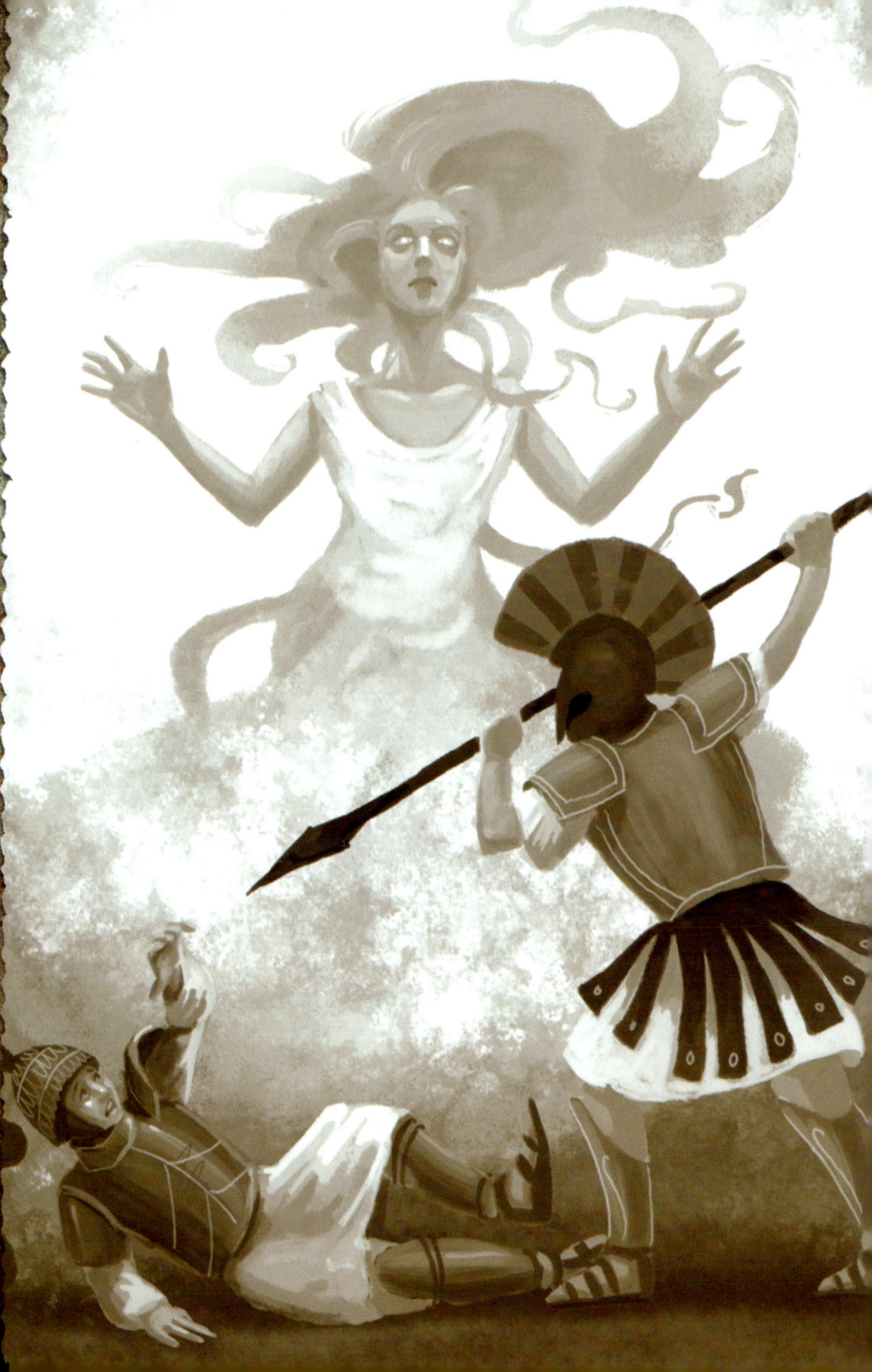

Menelaus is about to deal you a fatal blow. But a flash of light stops him. It is Aphrodite. She snatches you off the battlefield. Suddenly, you find yourself safely back in the palace.

"What have you done?" you ask, bewildered.

But she is already gone.

You're glad to be alive, but since you haven't finished your duel with Menelaus, the siege goes on. In the months that follow, you watch the battle rage from up on the battlements. Armed with a bow, you help defend the city.

Your brother Hector launches a daring attack to destroy the Greek ships. You watch him slay Patroclus, one of Greece's great heroes. But to your horror, he is then chased down by Achilles, Greece's mightiest warrior. Hector tries to defend himself, but he is killed right before your eyes.

Turn the page.

You grab an arrow and pull your bowstring back. You are determined to slay Achilles for killing your brother. You aim for his heart. But a strange voice changes your mind.

"Aim for his weak spot," a voice whispers in your ear. "Aim for his heel."

You do as you are told. Your arrow strikes Achilles in the heel. To your amazement, he is struck down.

While the battle ends with you slaying one of Greece's mighty heroes, it is a sad day. Your brother's planned attack failed. Worse yet, you saw him killed before your very eyes. With Hector's death, the Trojans lost their leader and eventually lose the war.

THE END

To follow another path, turn to page 13.
To learn about the real city of Troy, turn to page 105.

You doubt you could defeat the Spartan king, so you refuse his challenge. Your father is furious.

"Coward!" he shouts. "This war could be over!"

Ashamed, you leave the room to see Helen. But you only find your brother, Hector, in her quarters.

"Where is Helen?" you ask.

"I sent her back to King Menelaus," he says. "If you won't end this war, I will."

You rush to the window to see the Greek forces boarding their ships. The war is over.

But what of Aphrodite's promise? you think.

"If you won't fight for the one you love," you hear a voice whisper, "You don't deserve her."

THE END

To follow another path, turn to page 13.

To learn about the real city of Troy, turn to page 105.

You are glad to be alive, but you can't believe your mother asked you to leave Troy. This war is largely her fault. She had Paris steal Helen away. So, in a way, you feel responsible for defending the city. Besides, Hector's plan was working. The Trojan forces were driving toward the Greek ships.

You rush to rejoin the fight. To your surprise, the Trojan forces are now being pushed back. It all seems to be because of one man — Achilles.

You charge Achilles. The Greek hero appears unstoppable. Trojan after Trojan falls at his hands.

You hurl your spear at him, but it just bounces off. Then Achilles sets his sights on you. He charges. You are unable to avoid his spear thrust. He runs you through, and you fall to the ground.

THE END

To follow another path, turn to page 13.
To learn about the real city of Troy, turn to page 105.

You don't want to leave Troy when it seems you're about to win the war. But your mother is a goddess, so you trust her. You sail away from Troy. Soon after, you hear that the city has fallen to the Greek army. Aphrodite was right after all.

You sail east beyond the Aegean Sea. After a long journey, you land in Italy. There, you build a new kingdom, which will one day grow into the Roman Empire.

While the Greeks may have defeated the Trojans, your descendants will have revenge. The kingdom you start in Italy will spread across the known world. One day, it will conquer Greece and build a new city where Troy once stood.

THE END

To follow another path, turn to page 13.

To learn about the real city of Troy, turn to page 105.

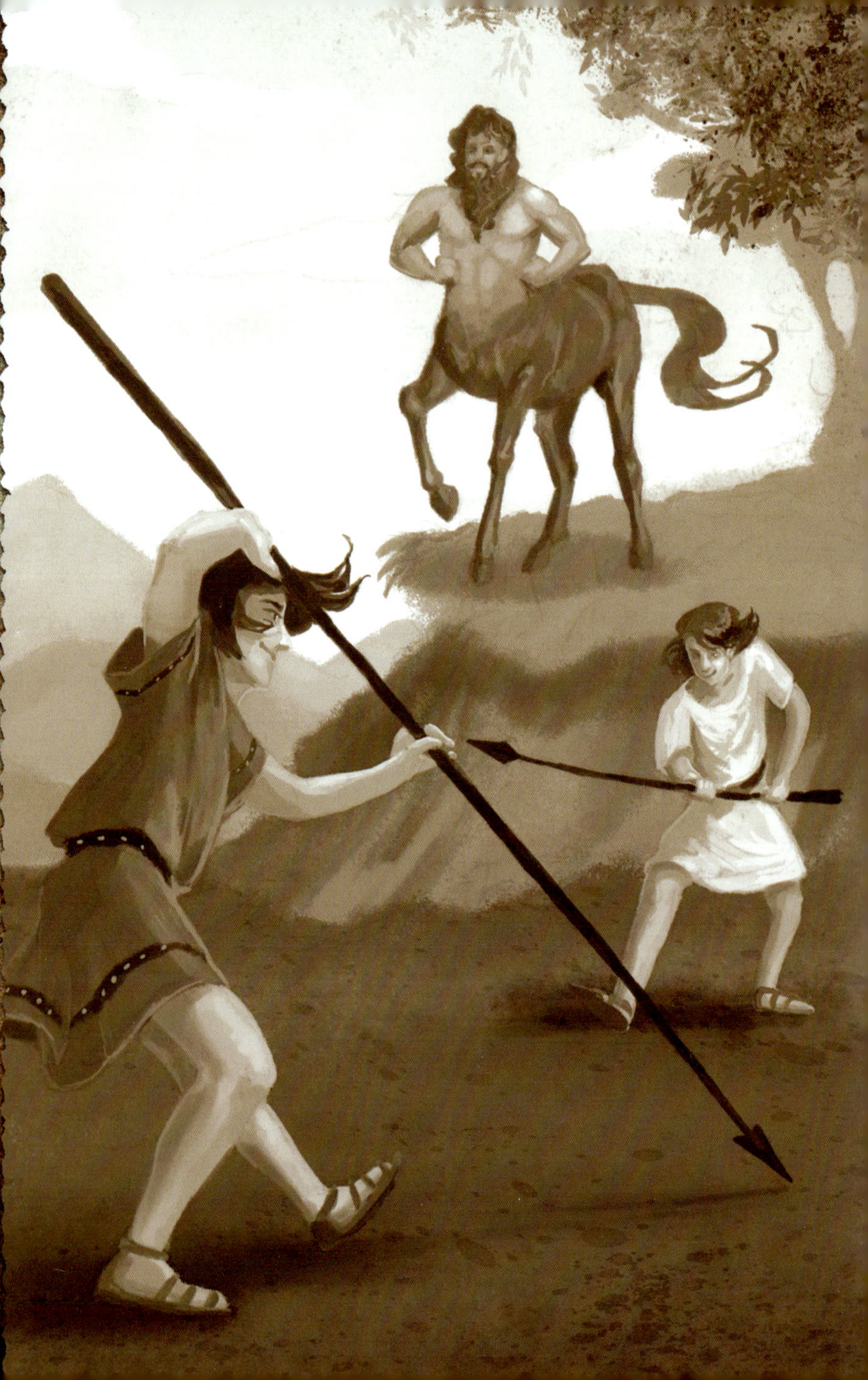

Chapter 3

Achilles and Patroclus

After their wedding, Peleus takes Thetis to his home in Phthia. There they have a son they name Achilles. Peleus and Thetis also raise Patroclus, the son of their friend Menoetius, as if he were their own.

Patroclus and Achilles grow up together as brothers. Achilles looks up to the older and wiser Patroclus. But Achilles is stronger and braver. Like Peleus, they both train with Chiron. This wise old Centaur teaches them battle skills that will be helpful on their adventures.

To be Achilles, turn to page 42.
To be Patroclus, turn to page 44.

Your mother, Thetis, has a gift of foresight. One day, while you are just a child, she tells you, "Underneath the battlements of Troy you will be slain by an arrow."

You are too young to understand what that means. But you can tell your mother is concerned for your safety.

"I have seen your death in a vision," she says. "But don't worry. I will find a way to keep you safe."

Your mother takes you to see your grandfather. Sitting on the shores of Lemnos, she tells Nereus of her vision.

"What shall I do, father?" she asks the sea god.

"Dip Achilles into the River Styx," he says. "Its waters will make him invulnerable to weapons."

The River Styx separates the world of the living from the Underworld. It has magical powers. The gods swear oaths upon it.

Your mother whisks you away to the banks of the River Styx. You stand on its rocky shore and look down at the dark water. You can't see what lies beneath the waves.

"But mother —" you protest, frightened.

"This is the best way for me to keep you safe," Thetis says. "Wherever the water covers you, you will be invulnerable."

To jump into the water yourself,
turn to page 47.

To have your mother dunk you in the water,
turn to page 50.

Your father was a mighty hero, as was your adopted father, Peleus. Your best friend, Achilles, is also a skilled warrior. So it is only natural that you train together for combat.

You earn a reputation as a brave warrior. But while Achilles will eventually rule his father's kingdom of Phthia, you are unsure of your future. You want a kingdom of your own.

Then one day, Achilles runs to you excited and says, "Helen of Sparta is choosing a husband."

"I've heard she is the most beautiful woman in the world," you reply.

Helen is the daughter of the Spartan King Tyndareus and Queen Leda. But rumor has it that her real father is the all-powerful Zeus.

"Then she deserves a mighty warrior such as yourself," Achilles says with a smile.

You blush. Like Helen, you are of marrying age. If the princess of Sparta becomes your wife, you might one day rule the famous city.

You arrive at Tyndareus's palace to find yourself among many princes and kings. They all want Helen as their bride. But Tyndareus is nervous about letting Helen choose a husband. You overhear him talking to the wise Odysseus.

"At some point Helen will have to choose," Odysseus says.

"I don't want to offend any of the kings or princes," Tyndareus replies. "I worry for the safety of my daughter and her future husband. What if one of the suitors is angry that he wasn't picked? He could start a war!"

"I have a plan," Odysseus says. He whispers something to Tyndareus.

Turn the page.

Later Tyndareus says to the suitors, "I will allow my daughter Helen to pick a husband, but only if you all swear an oath. You must agree to defend Helen's chosen husband in his time of need."

There is some grumbling, but the suitors all finally take the oath. Helen choses Menelaus, the brother of King Agamemnon of Mycenae.

Disappointed, you head home. Not long after returning, you receive horrible news. Helen has been taken by Paris, a prince of Troy. Menelaus sends word that he is raising an army to sail to Troy to free Helen.

To go fight with the Greek army, turn to page 52.
To go seek another adventure, turn to page 55.

"Okay, mother. I'll jump in," you say nervously, "But what if I see Charon?"

You've heard that for a price, Charon carries spirits of the dead across the River Styx.

"We aren't here to cross into the Underworld, so he is not waiting for us," your mother assures you. "Don't worry. Everything will be fine."

You shiver as your foot hovers above the dark water. Then you step forward. You expect to hit a muddy bottom just below the surface. But there is no bottom to this river. You plunge into the water, and the river swallows you in darkness.

You struggle to swim back to the surface. When you finally crawl onto the river's banks, your mother is gone. The land has turned darker than where you entered the river. You must have been swiftly carried downstream.

Turn the page.

Then you see a figure who frightens you. A ferry floats along the shore. It carries a dark-robed figure. He holds out a skeletal hand to you.

It is Charon, requesting payment for passage to the Underworld.

"But I'm not . . ." you begin to say. Then you look down at your hands. They are gray and misty, like those of a spirit.

I must have drowned in the river, you think.

You dig a coin out of your pocket. You place it in Charon's hand and step into his boat. He ferries you across the river to the Underworld, the land of the dead.

THE END

To follow another path, turn to page 13.
To learn about the real city of Troy, turn to page 105.

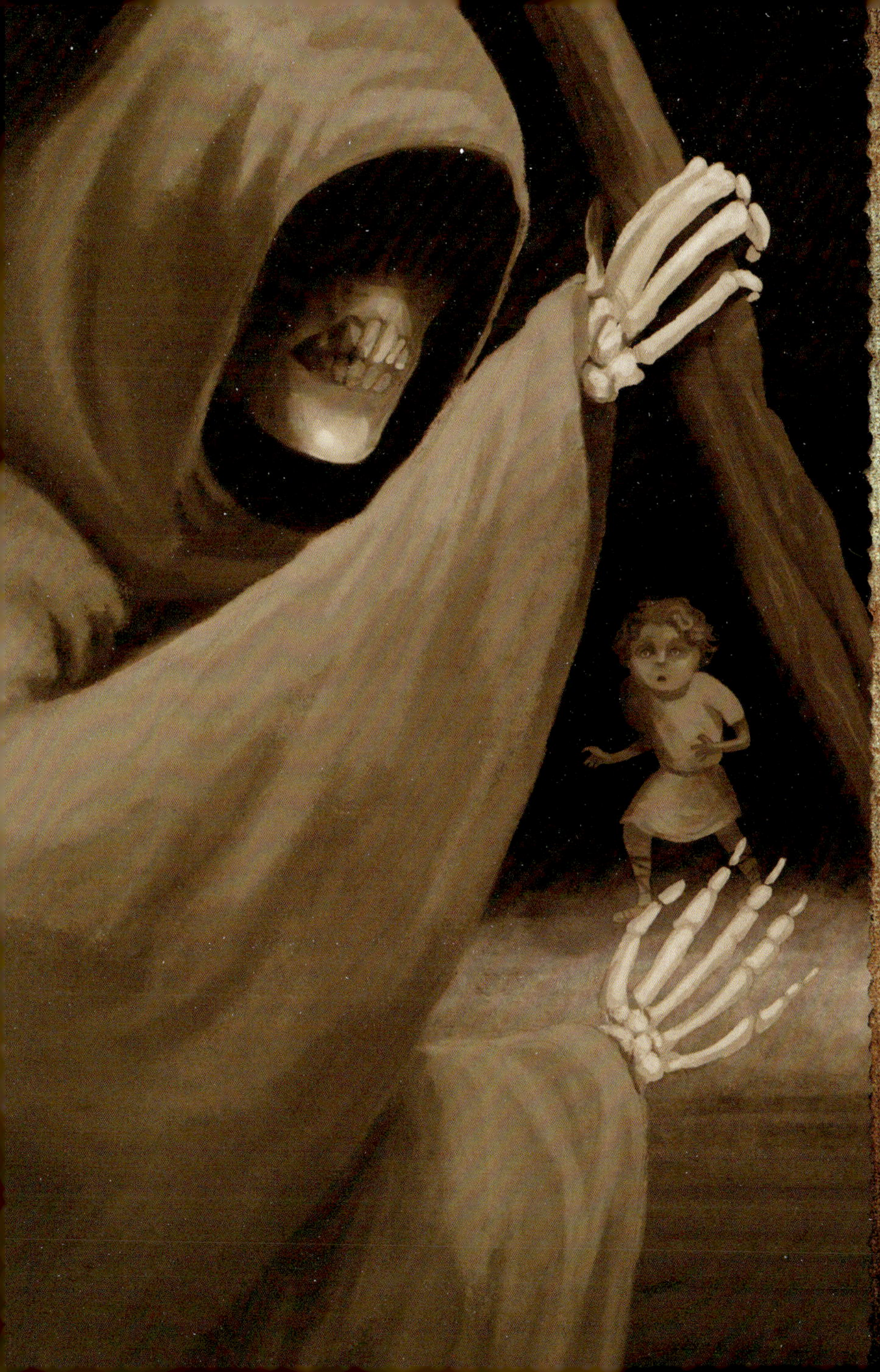

"I'm afraid," you tell your mother. "Can you hold onto me?"

"Of course," she says, picking you up.

She dips you into the river. Your mother holds your heel. It is the only part of you that it is out of the water. She pulls you out and tells you that no harm can come to you now. It must be true, for when you grow up, you win many battles and become famous throughout all of Greece.

Eventually your mother has another vision that you die in the kingdom of Troy.

"War is coming," Thetis warns. "I must hide you to keep you safe."

You let your mother disguise you as a woman. She sends you away to the island of Scyros, ruled by King Lycomedes. You live in his palace and pose as one of his daughters.

While in Scyros you hear that Paris, a Trojan prince, has stolen Helen from her husband, the Greek King Menelaus. He has raised an army to get her back.

A ship carrying Odysseus, the ruler of Ithaca, stops on Scyros on its way to Troy. You're afraid that Odysseus will have heard of you. But you don't think he recognizes you in your disguise.

Odysseus lays out gifts of weapons and treasure for the king. Suddenly a clash of swords rings out on the other side of the wall.

"We are under attack!" the king shouts.

"To arms!" Odysseus orders his men.

The soldiers rush toward the sound of battle.

To grab a weapon and help, turn to page 56.

To hide the treasure from the attackers, turn to page 59.

You swore an oath to defend Helen's chosen husband. If Menelaus is going to war, you feel you must help. You convince Achilles to join you.

You sail across the Aegean Sea to Troy. The Greek army has hundreds of ships. You can't imagine any city being able to withstand such a force. When you see the towering walls of Troy, you change your mind. Rumors say they were built by the gods Apollo and Poseidon.

The battle turns into a long war. One day, the Greeks have the advantage. The next day, the Trojans do. Achilles is the mightiest of the Greek heroes. His presence can change the tide of a battle. Many die fighting. But still, the Greeks fail to conquer the city of Troy.

After nine years of fighting, Achilles has had enough. He is angry with Agamemnon, commander of the Greek army.

"He doesn't honor the gods," Achilles says. "He has boasted that he is equal to Artemis in the skill of hunting. He has attacked Apollo's temple and captured one of his priests. No wonder the gods thwart us in our war against the Trojans."

Nothing you say can change his mind. Achilles stays in his tent as the war outside rages on.

Then the Trojans launch a massive attack. They force their way toward the shore where the Greek ships are anchored. If the Trojan army reaches them, they could burn your ships. You'd lose all of your supplies and have no way of getting home. The war would be lost.

Achilles has been Greece's mightiest warrior during the war. Without him, the army falters. Its forces are being driven back. So you head to Achilles's tent.

Turn the page.

"We need you now more than ever," you plead. "The Trojans will destroy our ships."

"This war has gone on too long already," he tells you. "I am done fighting."

Achilles was not one of Helen's suitors. He didn't vow to help Menelaus. Achilles is here because of you, but he is not obligated to fight.

"I understand this is not your war," you say. "But as my brother in arms, I ask for your help."

"What's mine is yours, brother," Achilles says. "Take my sword or my armor, and bring it back safely. But I will not fight for Agamemnon."

Your weapons and armor have been badly damaged in recent fighting. So you are thankful for Achilles's offer.

To take Achilles's sword, turn to page 60.
To take Achilles's armor, turn to page 62.

You do not want to go to war against Troy. You would rather go on a quest. You send word to Menelaus that you will not be joining him. When Achilles hears of your decision, he is disappointed.

"You swore to help Menelaus," he says.

"If he was under attack, I would go to his aid," you say. "But I didn't agree to wage war with him."

"Then I will take your place," Achilles says.

Those are the last words he speaks to you. Achilles joins Menelaus and sails to Troy. There he is slain by Paris, the prince who stole Helen.

Because you broke your vow, no other heroes will go on a quest with you. You live the rest of your life alone, in shame, and missing your best friend.

THE END

To follow another path, turn to page 13.
To learn about the real city of Troy, turn to page 105.

You are a warrior, and the home of your host is under attack. You instinctively rush toward the sounds of combat.

But when you burst through the doorway, what you see is not what you had expected. Odysseus stands with a wide smile. Behind him, several men clang swords against their shields.

"What's this?" you ask. "Where is the battle?"

"There is none," Odysseus says. "Just a trick to see through your disguise."

You realize you are standing in the middle of a group of soldiers, holding a spear and shield. But you are dressed as a princess. Patroclus walks up behind Odysseus. He laughs and asks you to join him on the battlefield.

You cannot deny your best friend. Despite what your mother wants, you head off to war.

The Greeks arrive on the shores of Troy with hundreds of ships and thousands of men. But the walls around the city are too strong to breach.

You quickly prove yourself a mighty warrior on the battlefield. Agamemnon, leader of the Greek army, sends you out to attack nearby towns. The towns can supply your army with food and more soldiers.

During one raid, you capture Princess Briseus. At first, she is afraid of you. After all, you are her captor. But you are kind to her, and she is smart and good-hearted. It is not long before the two of you fall in love.

"I will keep you safe," you promise. "When all this foolish fighting is over, we can return to Phthia and be married."

"I would like that," she says.

Turn the page.

Your happiness is short lived. Agamemnon has lost one of his servants who he had captured from Troy. She was the daughter of one of Apollo's priests, and the god demanded that Agamemnon return her to her father. He had no choice. But he is angry about it. In his anger, Agamemnon demands that you give him Princess Briseus to be his servant.

To refuse Agamemnon's request, turn to page 67

To give in to Agamemnon's request, turn to page 69.

Odysseus and his soldiers rush out the door. You could join them in defending the palace. But then you see the treasure left unguarded. Whoever is attacking the castle must be after it. You drag the chest to a hiding spot. You do not come out until after the sounds of battle end.

Afterward, King Lycomedes tells you Odysseus has sailed away. You don't end up going to war. Your mother's vision doesn't come true. But you find no happiness in cheating fate. You hear the war goes badly for the Greeks. Many Greek heroes are killed, including Patroclus, your dear friend.

The heroes that survive the war are bitter that you did not join them. So you end up living out your days on Scyros, with your mother.

THE END

To follow another path, turn to page 13.
To learn about the real city of Troy, turn to page 105.

"I will take your sword, then," you say.

"May the gods be with you," he replies.

Your chariot is outside Achilles's tent. You jump on, and your driver rushes you toward the battlefield. As you feared, Trojan soldiers surround the Greek ships. They could set them aflame at any moment. If they aren't driven back, the war will be over.

You raise your sword, shouting, "For Achilles!"

As you rush forward, there is a sudden change in the flow of the battle. Greek soldiers respond to your war cry.

"For Achilles!" they chant.

They are encouraged, thinking that their mightiest hero is about to join the fray. The Trojan soldiers falter and begin to fall back under the Greeks' newfound determination.

Suddenly a Trojan chariot turns toward you. It is Hector, commander of the Trojan army.

"Hold your ground," Hector shouts to his men. "It's not even Achilles."

Hector leaps from his chariot to face you. You do the same. He charges, jabbing at you with his spear. You knock the spear aside with your sword and go on the offensive. But Hector is too quick. He ducks and dodges your attacks. Then he lunges, burying his spear in your shoulder. You stagger back and collapse to the ground.

The last thing you see before you die is a group of Trojan soldiers setting fire to the Greek ships. You've lost your life, and it appears the Greeks have lost the war.

THE END

To follow another path, turn to page 13.
To learn about the real city of Troy, turn to page 105.

You quickly suit up in Achilles's armor.

Before you rush out of his tent, Achilles says, "Heed my warning. Defend the ships. But do not take the fight to Troy's gates, or one of the gods might feel the need to enter the battle."

You enter the battle dressed as Achilles. The Greek soldiers think that their mightiest hero has rejoined the fight. "For Achilles!" they chant. The Trojan soldiers think they are facing Achilles himself and flee from you.

You see two Trojan heroes before you. Sarpedon, who is a son of Zeus, and Hector, who is the leader of the Trojan army. Sarpedon stands his ground and Hector flees.

To face Sarpedon, go to page 63.
To chase after Hector, turn to page 64.

As Trojan soldiers flee before you, one man stands his ground.

"Why do you flee?" Sarpedon shouts. "Return to the battle, and I will challenge this man."

As you draw near Sarpedon, you leap off your chariot. He lunges with his spear. You dodge the blow and strike. But Sarpedon jumps aside.

Sarpedon attacks again. His spear connects with your armor. You stagger backward. But as Sarpedon moves in for another blow, he gives you an opening and you strike, driving your spear into his side. Sarpedon crumples to the ground.

You leap back onto your chariot. The Trojan forces continue to flee before you.

To chase after Hector, turn to page 64.
To return Achilles's armor, turn to page 66.

You order your driver to chase Hector. Defeating him will be a harsh blow to the Trojans. You leap out of your chariot and charge. Suddenly Hector cries, "Apollo, I seek your aid."

A brilliant light flashes before you. Dazed, you drop your spear and stagger backward. Hector quickly drives his spear into your side. You collapse to the ground and die.

Upon hearing of your death, Achilles rejoins the fight with a vengeance. He challenges Hector and kills him to avenge your death. You will not see your friend again until you meet in the Underworld, but you don't have long to wait. He also dies during the war. But your deaths are not in vain, because the Greeks win the war.

THE END

To follow another path, turn to page 13.

To learn about the real city of Troy, turn to page 105.

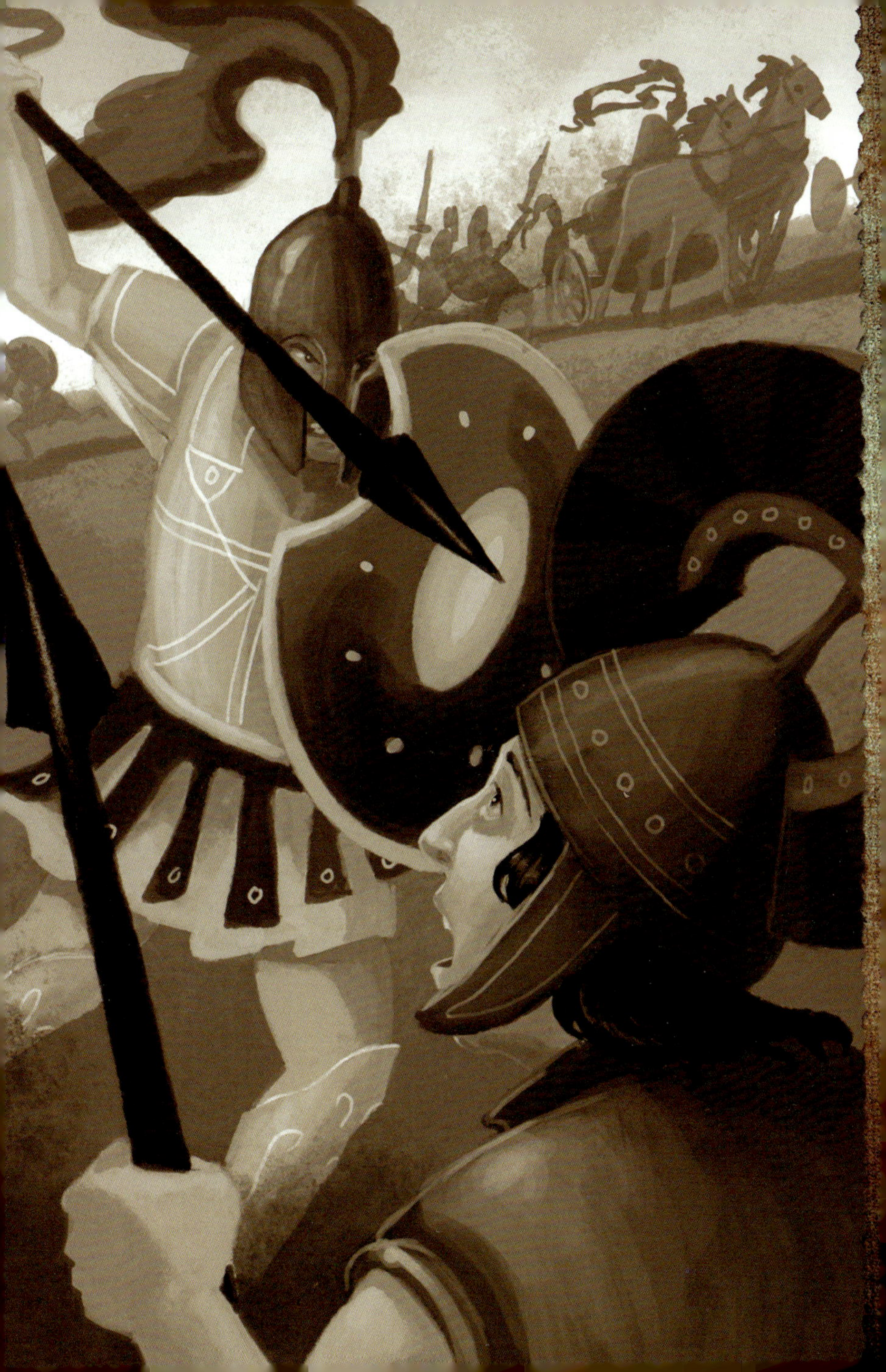

Achilles told you to return to him after defending the ships. You give Achilles his armor back, and he returns home.

The Greek soldiers lose confidence at the loss of their greatest hero. They also begin to doubt Agamemnon's leadership. The Greeks start to lose more battles than they win. You doubt Troy will ever fall. Eventually, Helen's former suitors meet. All but Menelaus agree to end the siege of Troy.

"This has gone on too long," Diomedes says.

"The war is lost," Odysseus announces. "Let us return to our families."

You agree and head home in defeat. Your only consolation is that you will see Achilles soon.

THE END

To follow another path, turn to page 13.

To learn about the real city of Troy, turn to page 105.

You and Briseus have just agreed to be married. You have fought valiantly for the Greek army. You do not deserve this treatment. You rush into Agamemnon's tent.

"You cannot ask for this," you say.

"No? Then I order it," Agamemnon replies.

"No!" you shout. "We are to be married."

Agamemnon laughs and draws his sword. You step back out of the tent and are surrounded by Agamemnon's guards.

You draw your sword as Agamemnon attacks. You block his blow and lash out at the nearest guard. You are greatly outnumbered, but you fight wildly. One by one, you cut down your attackers. But their blades bounce right off you.

Turn the page.

You are still outnumbered. Your only hope is to fight your way to one of the ships. As you flee, Agamemnon and his men chase after you. Patroclus and some of your other friends join the battle to defend you.

You make it safely to one of your ships. You set sail and flee. You've been driven from the battlefield. Not only did you lose Briseus, but Agamemnon spreads rumors that you are a traitor. It does not help that after your escape, the Greek army loses the war. Because of all this, you are no longer welcome in your homeland. For the rest of your life you and Patroclus live in exile. You never see your mother or father again.

THE END

To follow another path, turn to page 13.

To learn about the real city of Troy, turn to page 105.

Agamemnon is your commander. It breaks your heart, but you bring him Briseus. However, you will not fight for him anymore. Odysseus and Patroclus plead you to rejoin the fight, but you refuse. You do offer Patroclus your armor as protection.

You hear rumblings of lost battles and slain heroes. None of it bothers you — not until you learn that Patroclus has been slain by Hector, the Trojan commander. You are enraged when you hear the news. You storm into battle and see Hector leading the Trojan army.

"Hector!" you shout. Your voice rings out.

This is the moment the Greek forces have been waiting for — you rejoin the battle. The Trojans have feared this moment.

Turn the page.

You hack and slash away. Trojans fall before you, and the Greek army surges. Spears are hurled at you. Arrows rain down. You feel their stings, but they do not pierce your flesh.

"Hector!" you shout again, as you near the Trojan leader.

There is fear is his eyes. He flees, and you give chase. You catch him near the city's main gates.

Hector has no other choice. If he flees into the city, you and the Greek army will be able to follow and possibly conquer the city. So he spins around and hurls a spear at you. You dodge it. Then you pick up a spear from the battlefield and stab him with it. You bury the spear in Hector's side, and he collapses to the ground. All around you, the Greek army cheers.

Turn the page.

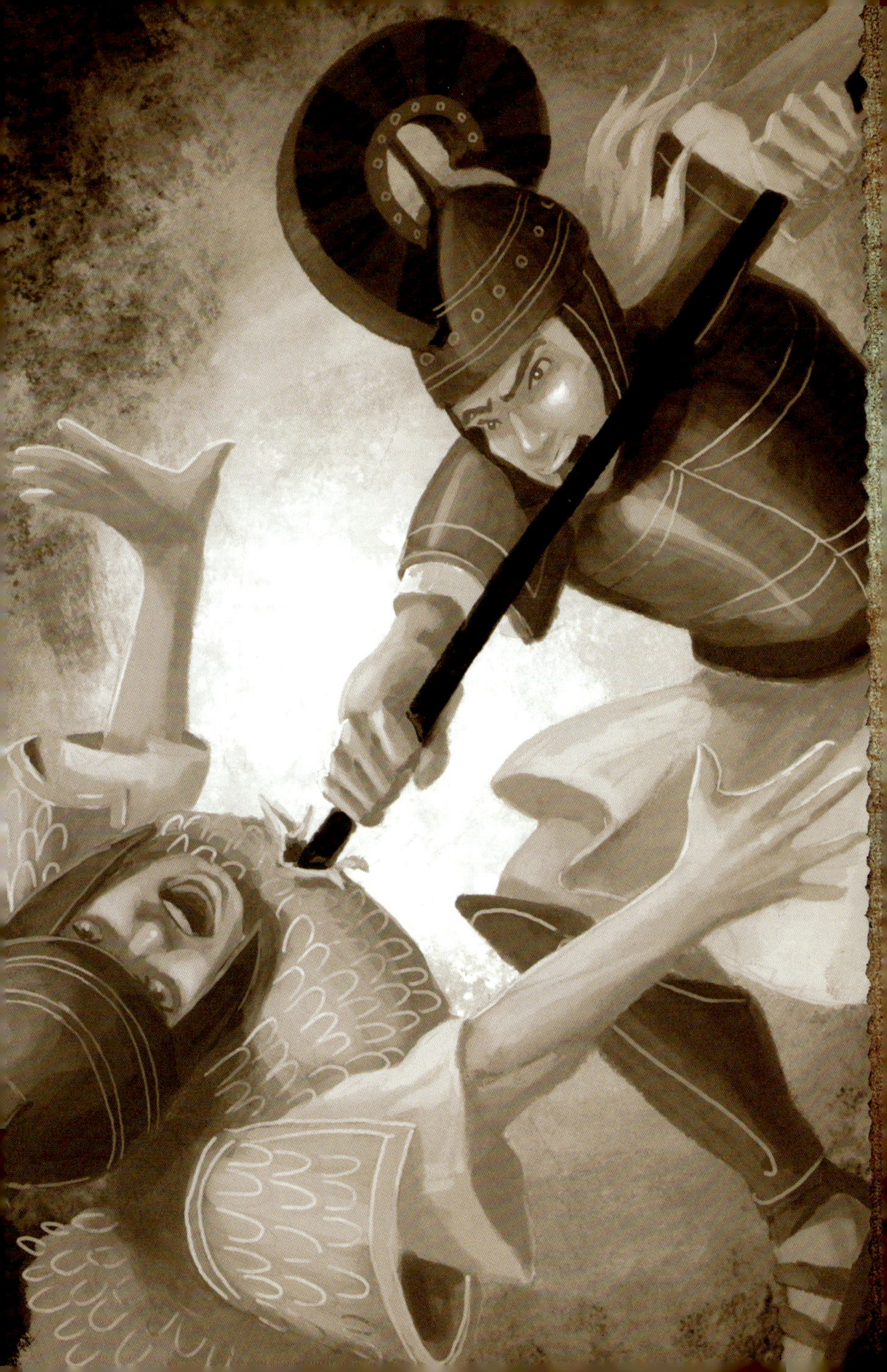

You have just defeated Troy's greatest hero. But all of a sudden you remember the words of your mother — you will die beneath the battlements of Troy.

THWIP!

An arrow flies through the air, fired by none other than Paris, prince of Troy. It strikes you in the heel, the only place you are vulnerable. It was the only part of you that wasn't dipped in the River Styx. You collapse to the ground in pain.

While it seems unlikely that you would die from such a wound, the magic protecting you everywhere else makes you very vulnerable where you were hit. There is nothing anyone can do to stop the bleeding from your wound. You bleed out and die right there on the battlefield.

You do not survive the war, but your legacy carries on. Stories will be told of your brave deeds for thousands of year.

Eventually the Greeks win the war, which they never could have done it without you.

THE END

To follow another path, turn to page 13.

To learn about the real city of Troy, turn to page 105.

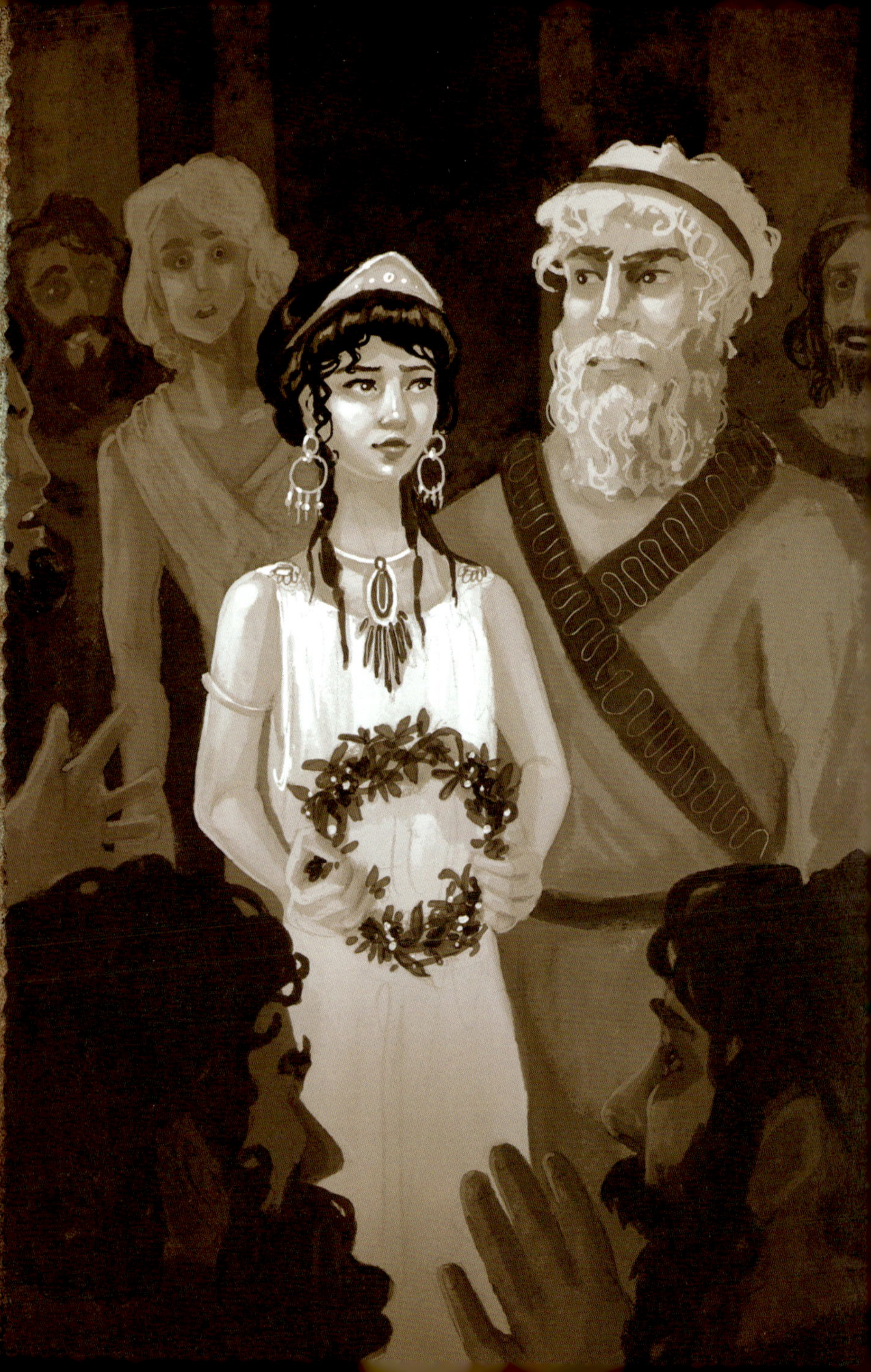

Chapter 4

The Heroes of Greece

The god Zeus has fathered children with several mortal women. Many of those children are mighty heroes. Zeus also has a daughter with Princess Leda. Her name is Helen, and she is the most beautiful woman in the world.

Because Zeus is a god and Leda a mortal, they cannot marry. After Helen's birth, Leda eventually marries King Tyndareus of Sparta.

When Helen becomes old enough to marry, suitors flock to Tyndareus's palace. Kings and princes from all over Greece want the princess's hand in marriage. Among them are two heroes, the wise Odysseus and the bold Diomedes.

Turn the page.

At first, Tyndareus will not let his daughter choose a husband. He worries for Helen and her future husband's safety. The suitors include many rival rulers. Tyndareus fears they might go to war if they cannot accept Helen's choice. Finally, he strikes a bargain with the suitors.

"You must all swear an oath," Tyndareus tells the men gathered at his palace. "You must pledge to protect Helen's husband from harm. Only then will I let her choose a husband."

Odysseus steps forward and swears the oath, as does Diomedes. Both heroes are highly respected. The other suitors follow their lead.

Helen then enters carrying a wreath of flowers. Slowly, she winds her way through the suitors and stands before Prince Menelaus. He is the brother of Agamemnon, king of Mycenae. Helen offers him the wreath.

"Helen is to wed Menelaus," Tyndareus says.

The other suitors return home. But not long after her wedding, Helen is kidnapped. Paris, a prince from Troy, steals her away. He brings her back to his kingdom and refuses to let her go.

Menelaus calls on all the suitors. They swore an oath to protect him as Helen's husband. He tells them to take up arms and to sail to Troy to help him win back his wife.

Menelaus's brother Agamemnon is chosen to lead the great Greek army that gathers. Odysseus and Diomedes are among his most trusted officers.

To be Odysseus, turn to page 78.
To be Diomedes, turn to page 81.

Your parents, King Laertes and Queen Antikleia, rule the island of Ithaca, off the coast of Greece. You have proven to be a brave leader so eventually your father steps aside, and you take the throne of Ithaca.

It was you who advised Tyndareus to make Helen's suitors swear an oath to protect her husband. But you actually had your eye on Tyndareus's niece, Penelope. As a reward for helping the king with the suitors, he gave you permission to marry her.

After Helen and Menelaus's wedding, you and Penelope marry. You return to Ithaca with your new wife. Soon after, you have a son, Telemachus. Wanting to know what the future holds, you find the seer Calchas. His words are heartbreaking.

"Do not sail east with the Greek army to wage war on the city of Troy," Calchas says.

"If you do," he continues, "the gods will keep you from returning home for many years. Your son will be grown and your home in ruins."

The next day, Menelaus knocks at your door. Penelope answers. You listen as Menelaus explains that his wife, Helen, has been kidnapped by Paris, a prince of Troy. He has refused to return her. So Menelaus is left with no other choice but to go to war with Troy.

You gasp. Calchas's words are coming true. The Greek army is sailing east to Troy, and you are expected to join them.

To try to hide from Menelaus, turn to page 83.
To go with Menelaus, turn to page 85.

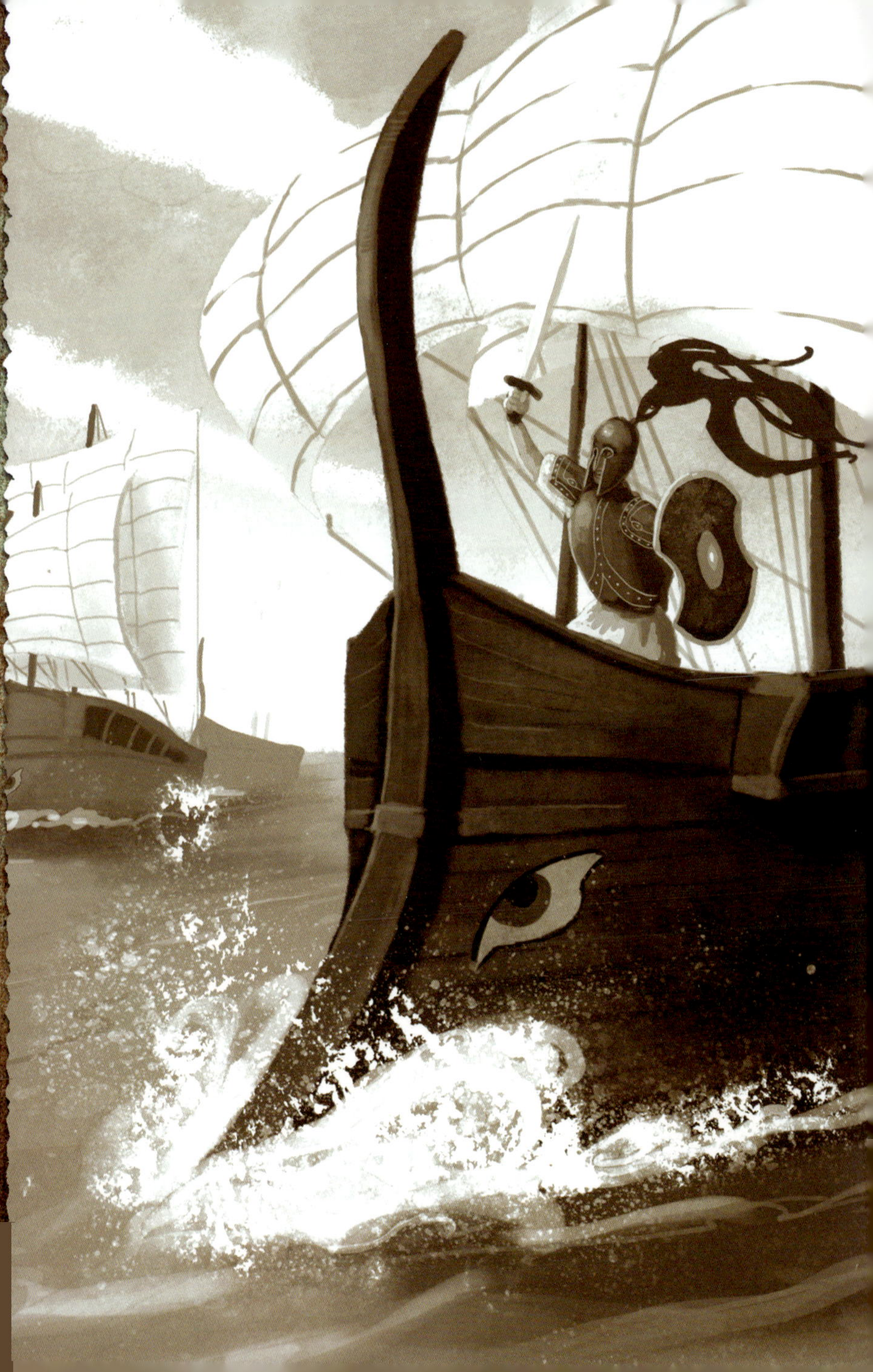

You are Diomedes, king of Argos. When Helen chose Menelaus to be her husband, you decided to marry Princess Aegiale instead.

When you hear Helen has been taken, you know it means war. You have 80 ships to add to the war effort. Situated on the Aegean Sea, Argos is the perfect staging point for the growing army. The number of ships grows into the hundreds. It is the mightiest Greek army ever assembled. You are confident as you set sail for Troy.

But even with such a large force, you can't break through the towering walls around Troy. Agamemnon, Menelaus's brother, is the leader of the Greek army. He orders a siege of the city.

You earn glory on the battlefield, but the siege lasts for years. You begin to wonder if the war will ever end.

Turn the page.

Then one day, after nine years of fighting, the Trojan army storms out of the city gates. You leap into battle. Spears whiz through the air. Swords clash. The Trojan army is charging toward your ships. If they set fire to them, all will be lost.

Suddenly you see a Trojan chariot charging at you. The rider hurls a spear, but you dodge it. You wait until the enemy's chariot is nearly upon you. Then you hurl your spear. It hits the driver in the chest. The chariot flips. Both Trojan soldiers fly from the vehicle. One of them quickly gets up and flees. The other doesn't move from the ground. Exhausted, you raise your sword to the sky. You call out for help from one of the gods.

To ask Athena, goddess of wisdom, for help, turn to page 95.

To ask Ares, god of war, for help, turn to page 98.

You think about what Calchas said — that you will be gone for many years if you sail to Troy. You decide to hide from Menelaus.

Your servant Eumaeus lives near your home. You know you can trust him. You run to his home and quickly tell him what Calchas said and how Menelaus has come for you.

"Hide here," he says. "I will go to your home and return once he leaves."

Eumaeus does not return until the next day. You can tell that something is wrong.

"Did Menelaus finally leave?" you ask.

"He did, after his soldiers searched your home and lands, my lord, but . . ." Eumaeus begins, "They have taken Penelope and your son."

"No!" you scream.

Turn the page.

Since you did not fulfill your oath, Menelaus takes your wife and son. They travel with him to Troy. You wait for their return, but the war lasts 10 long years. It is several more years before Menelaus reaches his home of Sparta.

You wait for word from your wife and son, but it never comes. It is not until you are old and dying that a young man comes to see you.

"Father? It is I, Telemachus," he says. "I'm here to tell you that Penelope, my mother, has died."

You are heartbroken at how your life has turned out. Even though you did not sail to Troy, Calchas's prophecy still came true.

THE END

To follow another path, turn to page 13.
To learn about the real city of Troy, turn to page 105.

You can't cheat your destiny or break your oath. You decide to go to war with Menelaus.

"Gather your forces and sail to Argos," he says. "We will gather there and set sail for Troy."

Calchas is going to Troy with the Greek army.

"Three tasks must be completed if this war is to be won," he tells you. "First, Thetis's son must join the fight. I will tell you the other two tasks when the time comes."

Thetis's son is Achilles. He is one of Greece's mightiest heroes. On the voyage to Troy, you stop at the island of Scyros. You have heard that Achilles is there. He was not one of Helen's suitors, but you plead with him to join the fight.

"The seer Calchas says the war cannot be won without you," you explain.

Turn the page.

"If I must," Achilles says, hanging his head.

You fear that, like you, he has also been told a prophecy about a sad fate should he sail to Troy.

You continue on to Troy. Even though the Greek army has gathered thousands of warriors, Troy is not easily taken. Its towering walls are rumored to have been built be the gods. And its army is nearly as strong as the Greeks.

The war wages on for many years, and Achilles is killed. Eventually Calchas tells you the second task that must be done for the Greeks to win the war — you must retrieve Hercules's bow.

Prince Philoctetes was with Hercules when the mighty hero died, so he may know where to find the bow. Philoctetes had sailed to Troy with you. But on the way, he was injured. Agamemnon told you to leave him behind on the island of Lemnos.

You sail to Lemnos and search for Philoctetes. It has been nine years since he was left behind. You're not sure he's even still alive. You find a cave that looks as though someone has been living there.

You hear a loud groan from the back of the cave. A figure dressed in rags shuffles into view. It is Philoctetes, limping from his old injury. He is armed with a bow and a quiver of arrows.

"Is that Hercules's famous bow?" you ask, pointing at his weapon. "The seer Calchas says the Greek army needs it to win the war."

"Yes. It was given to me by the mighty hero himself," he says. "And you cannot have it. It is my prized possession."

To take the bow from Philoctetes, turn to page 88.
To tell Philoctetes news of the war, turn to page 89.

Philoctetes is injured and bitter. You doubt that he will give you the bow. So you grab it.

"What treachery is this?" he shouts. "I curse you! Hercules's bow will only aim true for its rightful owner."

You ignore him and set sail back to Troy. But when you reach the battlefield, Philoctetes's curse holds true. Every arrow you shoot goes awry. You let Diomedes, Agamemnon, and Menelaus try, but no one can hit their targets.

Shortly after your return, Paris leads the Trojan army against you. With Achilles dead, the Greek army does not have the will to fight anymore. You are driven from Troy's shores, and the war is lost.

THE END

To follow another path, turn to page 13.

To learn about the real city of Troy, turn to page 105.

"The war is nearly lost," you say. "Achilles has been killed."

"Not Achilles," Philoctetes sighs, upset. "He was Greece's greatest hero, next to Hercules."

"He was slain by Paris, the prince who caused this war," you add.

"Then for Achilles," he shouts, puffing out his chest, "with this bow, I will seek revenge."

Philoctetes returns with you and quickly helps turn the war in Greece's favor. He even kills Paris using Hercules's bow.

Then Calchas tells you of the third task that needs to be completed before Troy falls.

"Steal the Palladium from Athena's temple," he says, "This wooden statue protects the city."

Turn the page.

Disguised as beggars, you and Diomedes sneak into Troy and take the Palladium from Athena's temple. You then seek out the seer to ask if there is anything else you should do.

"Make a hollow offering to the people of Troy," Calchas says. "If they accept, Troy will fall."

You think about Calchas's words. Troy's walls cannot be breached. But you and Diomedes snuck into the city in disguise. Could you sneak a group of soldiers into the city too? The hollow offering will be the perfect disguise.

You want to keep favor with the gods, so you decide to shape the offering into an animal that would please them.

To build a statue of an animal sacred to Athena, go to page 91.

To build a statue of an animal sacred to Poseidon, turn to page 92.

The Palladium was a gift from the goddess Athena. Her sacred animal is the owl. Your soldiers build a large wooden owl and roll it up to Troy's main gate. You hide inside with some of Greece's best soldiers. Outside, the Greek army sails away. Soldiers from Troy open the main gate. They see the large wooden statue.

"The Greeks have gone," a soldier says. "This must be a peace offering.

"Athena has forsaken us," argues a priest named Laokoon. "We should burn the statue."

You smell smoke and see flames creeping into the statue. The soldiers try to escape, but anyone who gets out is struck down by the Trojans. Everyone inside the statue dies, including you.

THE END

To follow another path, turn to page 13.

To learn about the real city of Troy, turn to page 105.

Poseidon, the sea god, is an important figure to the people of Troy. He also helped build the walls that protect the city. So building a large statue of a horse, his sacred animal, seems fitting.

Out of sight from the Trojans, your men build a large wooden horse. Then one night, you roll it up to the main gate. You hide inside with some of Greece's best soldiers. Outside, the Greek army sails out of sight. The Trojans will think you have given up on the war.

The next day, soldiers from Troy open the main gate. They see the large wooden statue.

"This must be a peace offering," a soldier says.

"We should bring it inside," another says.

A Trojan priest named Laokoon warns, "Be wary of Greek trickery."

Turn the page.

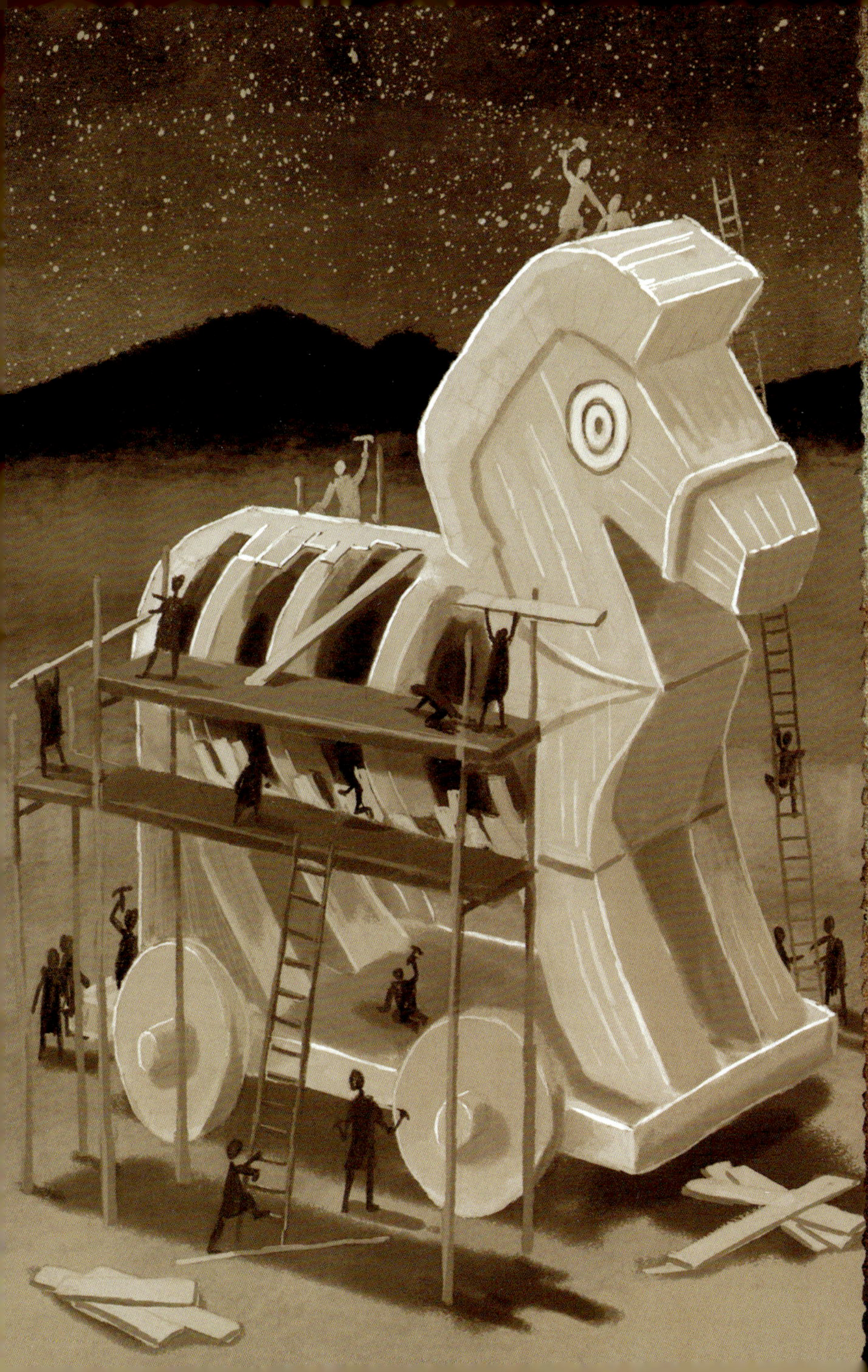

Then you hear a scream coming from outside the horse. One of Poseidon's sea serpents has snatched up Laokoon. With that, the Trojan soldiers roll the horse inside.

You and the soldiers wait until night falls. Then you sneak out of a trap door in the bottom of the statue. You head toward the city gates. During the night, the Greek army had sailed back and snuck up to the gates. Once you open them, the soldiers charge inside.

The Trojans are caught off guard by the invading Greeks. After the long siege, Troy finally falls.

The war is over, and you helped win it. Now you begin the long voyage home to your family.

THE END

To follow another path, turn to page 13.
To learn about the real city of Troy, turn to page 105.

"Wise goddess," you shout. "Grant me the strength to continue this fight."

The goddess must have heard your call for help. Suddenly, you feel full of strength. Not only is Athena the goddess of wisdom, she is also the protector of heroes. And this day, she favors you. You grab a spear and charge into battle.

You fling the spear at one Trojan, striking him in the chest. Then you lash out with your sword, cutting down another Trojan. Athena's support pushes the Greek soldiers to fight harder. The Trojan forces are driven back to the city's gates.

Suddenly, a Trojan chariot approaches you. In it you spy Aeneas. He is one of Troy's greatest heroes and rumored to be the son of Aphrodite.

"Diomedes," shouts a friend, "You are wounded. You are no match for Aeneas."

Turn the page.

"The tide of the battle is turning," you say. "I need to make sure the day's battle is won."

You charge toward Aeneas as he hurls a spear at you. You block it with your shield and hurl your spear at his chariot driver. You hit him, and he loses control. Aeneas is flung from the chariot.

You draw your sword and rush to end the Trojan hero. Just as you are about to deal him a fatal blow, a brilliant white light flashes. It is the goddess Aphrodite, come to save her son.

"No!" you shout. You lash out with your sword, striking the goddess across the wrist. She cries out and backs away.

"Goddess of love, you have no place on the battlefield," you say.

"And love shall have no place in your life," she yells at you. "How dare you attack a god!"

Suddenly Aphrodite and Aeneas disappear from the battlefield.

You are shaken. But you have little time to think about it. Suddenly, you hear another soldier shout, "Hector has joined the battle!"

Hector is Troy's mightiest hero. Many Greeks have died at his hands. This is your chance to avenge them.

You rush to attack, but stop when you see Ares, the god of war, driving Hector's chariot. He is urging the Trojans on and is the reason Hector is such an unstoppable force.

If I don't stop him, the battle will be lost, you think. But Aphrodite has just warned you against challenging a god. What should you do?

To retreat, turn to page 100.

To attack Hector, turn to page 102.

"Ares, god of war," you shout. "I call upon you to see me victorious in this battle."

Suddenly, you feel a burst of strength and a crazed desire to fight. You leap into your chariot and see that Ares has taken the driver's seat. He flashes you a wicked grin, and speeds the chariot into the thick of battle.

Ares smashes the chariot into the Trojan forces. Then you start hacking wildly with your sword. Many Trojans fall as Ares urges you on. You don't see the fear in the eyes of the soldiers you face. You don't even notice your own wounds. Spears are hurled in your direction. Arrows pierce your armor. Still, you fight on, screaming "For Ares! For Ares!" until the Trojan forces flee from you.

You saved the day. The ships are safe. But at what cost?

Once the city gates close and the surviving Trojans are safe behind their city's walls, Ares leaves you. That is when you notice the damage to your body. You have been cut and pierced and are bleeding from wounds too numerous to count.

Another Greek soldier rushes to your side. "The battle is won!" he shouts.

His rejoicing falters as you collapse to the ground. Your body has suffered too much to survive.

THE END

To follow another path, turn to page 13.

To learn about the real city of Troy, turn to page 105.

We must retreat, you think. *Perhaps we can regroup around the ships and prevent the Trojans from reaching them.*

You leap into your chariot. Your driver wheels it around.

"Retreat to the ships!" you shout.

The Greek army retreats frantically toward the ships, and the Trojans chase them furiously. You had hoped you could form a defensive line around the ships to hold off the Trojans. But under the influence of Ares they are unstoppable. They smash through your defenses, cut down your soldiers, and make their way to the ships. Most of your remaining forces have scattered. Your heart sinks as you realize that the battle is all but lost.

To your horror, you see the first ship set ablaze. And then another, and another. Soon, the shoreline is lit up by the flames of your burning vessels.

Your supplies are lost, as is your way home. With this defeat, the Greek army loses all desire to fight on.

You surrender and are taken prisoner. You wait for your wife to send ransom money for your release. But it never comes. You die imprisoned in Troy's dungeon.

THE END

To follow another path, turn to page 13.

To learn about the real city of Troy, turn to page 105.

To face Ares is certain death. Hercules is the only mortal who has ever survived after facing him in battle. But what choice do you have? Your troops are being cut down before your eyes.

You leap into your chariot, and in your driver's place stands Athena.

"My brother Ares has no right to be on this battlefield," she shouts. Then your chariot lunges forward. You race toward Hector and Ares.

Ares turns Hector's chariot toward you. In one hand he holds the reins. In the other, he wields a spear, which he hurls in your direction. Athena plucks it out of the air.

As Hector's chariot rushes past, you thrust your spear at Ares, and he screams in pain. Then he disappears from the battlefield, never to return. In the next instant, Athena also is gone.

You are left alone, standing in your chariot, as the Greek army chases the Trojans back inside their city. The battle is won!

Your victory has encouraged the Greek army, while disheartening the Trojan forces. Soon after, the war is won. The city of Troy is sacked. After retrieving Helen, Menelaus heads home with the Greek forces.

Upon your return to Argos, your elation from winning the war turns to sadness. Your wife is gone. Then you recall wounding Aphrodite on the battlefield. You survived a great war, but in the end, the goddess of love has her revenge. She has taken love from your life.

THE END

To follow another path, turn to page 13.

To learn about the real city of Troy, turn to page 105.

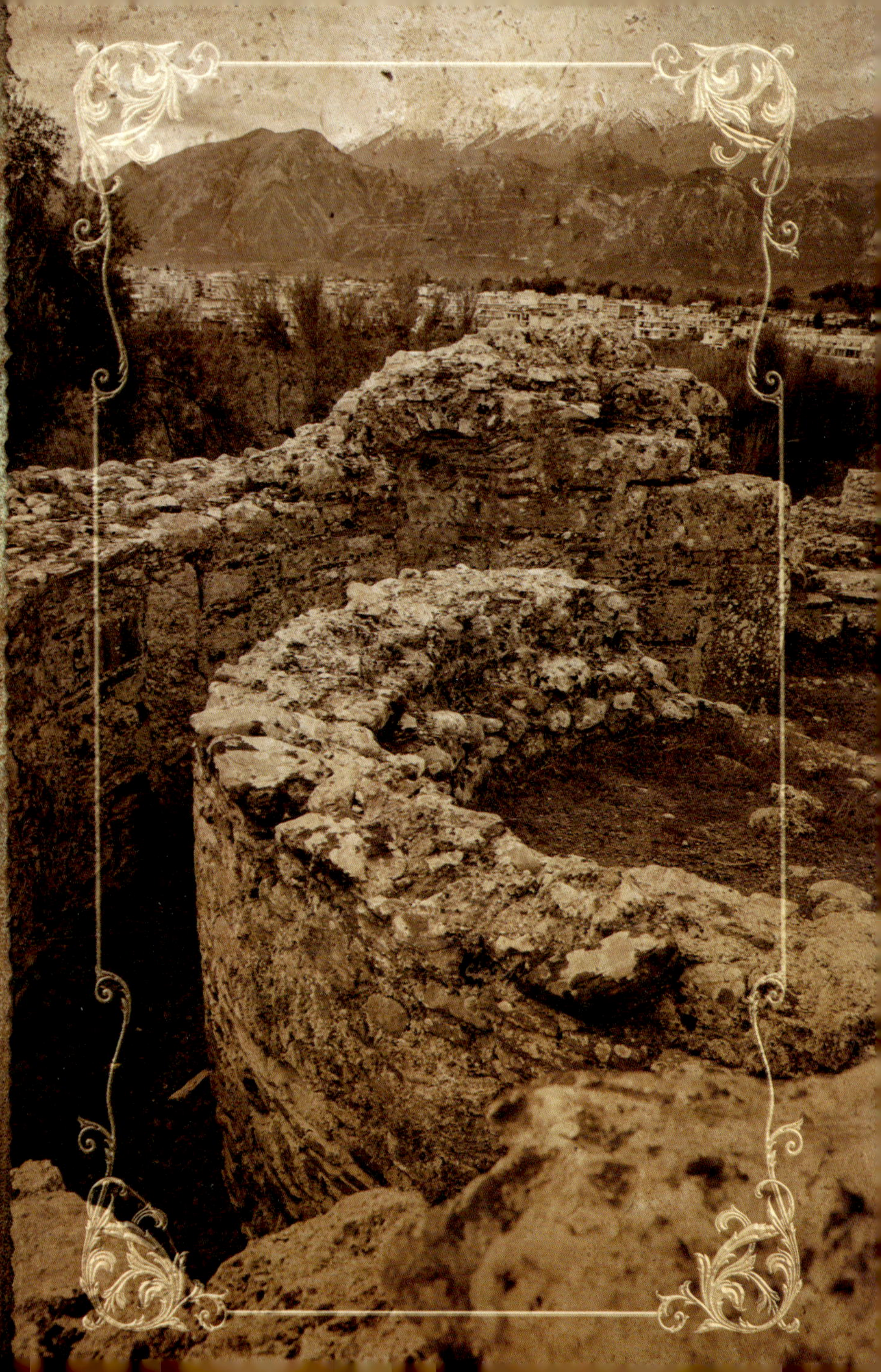

Chapter 5

The Real City of Troy

The story of the Trojan War is one of the best-known Greek myths. It centers on the Trojan prince Paris stealing Helen away from her husband, King Menelaus. The Greek army eventually wins the war by tricking the Trojans into letting them into the city in a wooden horse.

But did the city of Troy actually exist? In the 1870s, German archaeologist Heinrich Schliemann unearthed the ruins of what many think was the ancient city of Troy.

The original Troy was a small village founded around 3000 BC. It eventually grew into a thriving city.

Turn the page.

When the Trojan War was believed to have occurred, the city was at its peak of wealth and power. To date, archaeologists have not found evidence of a large-scale war. But they have found spear tips and arrowheads embedded in the city's walls. These show signs of numerous small conflicts. There is believed to have been continued unrest and rebellion over a period of time, which might be the source for the stories of a long drawn-out war.

Today, the site where Troy once sat is now a tourist attraction. People from all over the world come to see a replica of the Trojan Horse. They tour ruins of the ancient city and marvel over stories of mighty heroes and powerful gods. Though the city was destroyed hundreds of years ago, myths surrounding it continue to entertain people of all ages.

Greek Gods and Goddesses

Aphrodite—goddess of love, desire, and beauty; she enjoyed tricking gods into falling in love with mortals

Apollo—god of music; son of Zeus and twin brother to Artemis

Ares—god of war and son of Zeus and Hera

Artemis—goddess of purity and the moon; known as a huntress; daughter of Zeus and twin sister to Apollo

Athena—goddess of wisdom and daughter of Zeus

Eris—goddess of chaos and strife; Zeus's daughter and known as a troublemaker

Hera—goddess of marriage and childbirth; wife of Zeus

Hermes—messenger of the gods and son of Zeus

Nereus—water god also known as the Old Man in the Sea; father of Thetis

Poseidon—god of the sea and Zeus's brother. Poseidon was strong-willed and had a bad temper.

Thetis—a sea goddess and Nereid; one of the 50 daughters of the Old Man in the Sea

Zeus—god of the sky and ruler of the Greek gods. He was known for trying to be just and fair.

OTHER PATHS TO EXPLORE

1. Imagine Paris had actually given the golden apple to Athena and received her gift of becoming a great warrior. What adventures might he have had? How would he have fared against the Greek heroes mentioned throughout this story?

2. When Diomedes needs help, he calls upon Athena, goddess of wisdom and the protector of heroes. She supported the Greeks because Paris awarded the golden apple to Aphrodite. But what might have happened if Diomedes called upon Hera? How would the queen of the gods, Zeus's wife, have helped Diomedes in battle?

3. There are several reasons mentioned in the story for why Achilles gets upset with Agamemnon and quits the battlefield. This eventually leads to Patroclus and Achilles dying. But how might things have happened differently if Achilles had kept fighting despite what Agamemnon did?

Read More

Chandler, Matt. *The Trojan War: A Graphic Retelling.* Graphic Myths. North Mankato, Minn.: Capstone Press, 2017.

Hoena, Blake. *Epic Adventures of Odysseus: An Interactive Mythological Adventure.* You Choose Greek Myths. North Mankato, Minn.: Capstone Press, 2017.

Spies, Karen Bornemann. *Mythology of the Iliad and the Odyssey.* Berkeley Heights, NJ: Enslow Publishers, Inc., 2015.

Internet Sites

FactHound offers a safe, fun way to find Internet sites related to this book. All of the sites on FactHound have been researched by our staff.

Here's all you do:
Visit *www.facthound.com*
Type in this code: 9781515748229

GLOSSARY

breach (BREECH)—to break open a gap in a wall

Centaur (SEN-twar)—a half-man, half-horse creature

chariot (CHAYR-ee-uht)—a two-wheeled vehicle pulled by horses and used in ancient battles

mortal (MOR-tuhl)—human, referring to a being who will eventually die

Nereid (NAYR-eed)—a sea nymph; Thetis is one of the 50 Nereid, who are all daughters of the sea god Nereus

Olympian (oh-LIM-pee-uhn)—one of the 12 Greek gods who ruled the world from Mount Olympus

Palladium (pu-LAY-dee-uhm)—a statue of Athena

prophecy (PRAH-fuh-see)—a foretelling of something that might happen in the future

seer (SEE-uhr)—a person who can see the future

siege (SEEJ)—a military strategy in which an army surrounds a city or fort, hoping to force it to surrender

suitor (SOO-tuhr)—someone who seeks to marry someone else